OLD YORKSHIRE DALES

The Cover Photograph: John Edenbrow

Also available in the David & Charles Series

THE SOMERSET & DORSET RAILWAY – Robin Atthill
THE COUNTRYMAN WILD LIFE BOOK –
Bruce Campbell (Editor)
BUYING ANTIQUES – A. W. Coysh and J. King
INTRODUCTION TO INN SIGNS – Eric R. Delderfield
THE CANAL AGE – Charles Hadfield
THE SAILOR'S WORLD – Captain T. A. Hampton
OLD DEVON – W. G. Hoskins
LNER STEAM – O. S. Nock
THE WEST HIGHLAND RAILWAY – John Thomas
BRITISH STEAM SINCE 1900 – W. A. Tuplin
RAILWAY ADVENTURE – L. T. C. Rolt

The David & Charles Series

———————

OLD YORKSHIRE DALES

———————

ARTHUR RAISTRICK

UNABRIDGED

PAN BOOKS LTD : LONDON

First published 1967 by David & Charles (Publishers) Ltd.
This edition published 1971 by Pan Books Ltd,
33 Tothill Street, London, S.W.1

ISBN 0 330 02739 5

Printed in Great Britain by
Cox & Wyman Ltd, London, Reading and Fakenham

Contents

Illustrations in Photogravure

Acknowledgements

The author wishes to acknowledge the following for the use of their photographs: Bertram Unné, C. Crossthwaite, G. Hollingshead and A. Raistrick.

List of Line Drawings

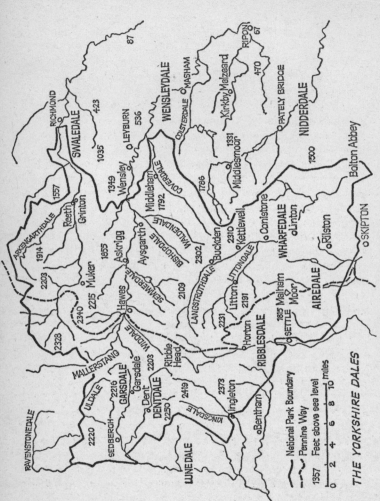

Fig 1. Outline map of Yorkshire dales

CHAPTER ONE

The Yorkshire dales

THE PENNINES extend as a mountain area from near Derby to the Tyne valley, about 140 miles from south to north, and they will be remembered by many from the schoolbooks of their youth as the 'Backbone of England'. As every child was expected to know, they are divided by the through valley of the Aire Gap into two nearly equal parts and the northern half is again divided by the Stainmore Pass into the Yorkshire dales and the Durham and Northumberland dales with a bit of Cumberland in the north-west. A fourfold division is completed by regarding the Pennines south of the Aire Gap as consisting of the Derbyshire hills and the south Yorkshire moors.

The Yorkshire dales can be defined conveniently as the Pennine dales between the Aire and Stainmore, or in the last few years as the Yorkshire Dales National Park with the addition of Nidderdale and a small margin on the east to extend to the foot of the Pennines where the dales open out to the Vale of York (Fig 1). Yorkshire has a wonderful river system which drains nearly the whole county by the Humber and its two main tributaries, the Ouse and the Trent, with the Ribble and Lune to drain the western slopes of the Pennines to the Irish Sea. The dales of this book consist of the upper parts of the valleys of the Aire, Wharfe, Nidd, Ure, and Swale, all draining eventually into the Humber, with the upper Ribble and the tributaries of the Lune, which are the Rawthey, Clough, Dee, Greta, and upper Wenning, running to the west. The great pass of Stainmore is drained by three rivers, Greta, Balder, and Lune, all tributaries of the Tees, and here we notice what is a common feature in the north, the frequent duplication of river names, in this case the Greta and Lune. On its north side

the pass rises quickly to the flanks of Mickle Fell, the highest
peak in Yorkshire, 2,591 ft Ordnance Datum, and in the south
merges with the fells on the north side of Swaledale.

A useful artificial boundary to the area in which we are interested can mostly be defined by modern roads (Fig 2). The
trunk road A65 through Skipton and Settle to Kirkby Lonsdale
is used as the southern boundary of the National Park and we
will adopt it also. As we approach the Lune near Kirkby Lonsdale we can turn north along A683 to Sedbergh, a road along
the east side of the Lune which varies little from the line of the
Roman road through Casterton, and from Sedbergh we can
continue along the Roman road, now Fairmile Lane, along the
west side of the Howgill Fells. At a point between Lowgill and
Low Borrowbridge (a Roman station) and five miles beyond
Sedbergh, the boundary between Yorkshire and Westmorland
leaves the Lune and turns east up Carlin Gill and so across the
summit of the Howgills, then by Rawthey Bridge and Uldale
over Swarth Fell to Mallerstang. It then runs north along the
summit of Mallerstang Common, north-east to near Tan Hill,
then north again to cut the A66 road over Stainmore near Rey
Cross and the Roman Camp. A66 is the road across the length
of Stainmore, eagerly watched and reported in the Press along
with the road over Shap Fell as being one of the earliest and
most frequently blocked by snow. Tales of lorries and cars
snowed up and abandoned on Stainmore are a commonplace
in any severe winter, and indeed a winter without such a
blockage would in itself be almost sensational news.

We follow A66 to the east as far as Bowes and then on to
Rokeby and Greta Bridge, where it turns south-east to join the
A1 at Scotch Corner. A1, another Roman road – the Leeming
Lane through Catterick – is a convenient boundary which we
follow south for twenty miles and then leave it by A61 through
Ripon to Harrogate, then west and slightly south by A59 to
our starting point at Skipton, part of A59 being a Roman road.
Thus more than half the boundary is framed by Roman roads,
a reminder that the dales are indeed the heart of Brigantia,
whose natives the Romans tried to 'contain' within a circuit of
roads and forts of which this is a substantial part.

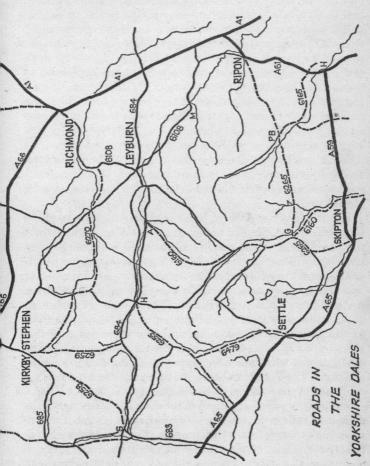

Fig 2. Map of roads in the Yorkshire Dales

If we think in terms of geology and topography this area, except for the Howgill Fells, can be looked upon as a single unit and is now generally known as such by the name of the 'Askrigg Block', Askrigg being near to the centre. It can be visualized in very general terms as a block of country tilted towards the east and having a 30-mile-long and fairly gentle slope to the Vale of York on the east and a shorter 10-mile slope to the valley of the Lune on the west. Along the high north to south ridge between these two slopes the fells are nearly all 100 or 200 ft more than 2,000 ft O D and indeed, within the area we have just defined, there are over thirty summits over 2,000 ft, including such famous hills as Ingleborough, Peny-gent, Whernside, Great Shunner Fell, and others (Illus. 2). This high ground accounts for about a third of the whole area, and more than two-thirds is above 1,000 ft O D. On the east-ward slope the 1,000-ft contour is frequently less than 10 miles west of the A1.

The whole of the Askrigg Block is composed of rocks of the Carboniferous Series, the Great Scar Limestone, with above it the Yoredale Series and then the Millstone Grit. Because of the tilt of the whole block the Great Scar Limestone is the domi-nant rock of the west and south-west and forms the wonderful limestone scenery of Craven. As the dales are crossed to the north and east the Yoredale Series of alternations of limestones, shales and sandstones become more prominent and it is from Wensleydale (Yoredale is an old and alternative name for this valley) that the series is named. In the east and north-east the dip of the rocks has generally carried the Great Scar Limestone and part of the Yoredales below the valley floor and the fells are composed of the rough grits and shales of the Millstone Grit.

The general physical pattern of the dales can be thought of as a group of valleys cut into a massive mountain plateau, often to a depth of 1,000 ft below the summits. The dales are narrower than the long lines of moorland which separate them from one another, so that to travel from a village in one dale to one in the next may mean a moorland journey of five or ten miles. There are not many roads across the moors and to go by car from one dale to the next can mean a journey of several miles up or down the valley to get to the beginning of the moorland road. This is one way in which the rambler has the advantage, as he can cross directly over the moor or go by any of the green roads and bridleways remaining from the days of the drovers. This pattern has imposed a lengthwise movement along the dales, so that in most things the communities in different dales are still separate.

The geological differences are reflected in colour, for this is a colourful country. In the south-west the soft and almost perennial green of the limestone turf and the grey to white of the limestone crags and dry stone walls blend miraculously to a symphony of grey-green which no other type of country can provide. The stark limestone features are softened and often relieved by the yews which grow on the high rock faces. There is no great difference between summer and winter colours, except that the benty grass of the higher slopes takes on a lighter colour in autumn, but this does little to affect the general grey-green picture. Trees are not an important part of the landscapes, except for the scrub wood of thorn and ash which commonly thrives on the screes below the limestone scars, and for the rare plantation. The intensity of sheep-grazing ensures that there is no material regeneration of woodland on the upland pastures. A feature of the limestone country is the limestone pavements, great areas, often scores of acres of bare limestone, carved into an intricate reticulation of deep solution channels along the joints (grikes) separating the blocks (clints) of remaining limestone. In the grikes there is a rich flora of ferns and many former woodland plants, mute evidence of the time before the clearance of forest cover by early man and his grazing animals (Illus. 3).

The country of the Yoredales, Wensleydale in particular, is of a richer green and is more varied. The valleys are wider, the farmland is more frequently divided by hedgerows, and woodland plantations are more abundant. The picture is of stronger colours and more variety – the sandstones in the upper Yoredales are thicker and heather moors creep down the upper slopes. This is nearer the norm of any rich countryside, with Craven varying into the softer grey-green and Swaledale to the north being altogether darker. In Swaledale limestone, except at the head around Muker and Keld (Illus. 4), is far less obvious than in the other dales and the prime feature of the hills is their heather cover, därk brown to black except when in flower, when its purple splendour sets it apart from all except parts of upper Nidderdale. The more abundant bracken adds an element of bright green, changing to russet and red-brown in the winter scene, that is absent in the limestone dales (Illus. 5).

In the north-west – the Howgills, Dentdale and Garsdale – the velvety green of the summer fells turns to more sombre winter colours, but the vast expanses of unenclosed and unbroken fellsides make this an area where the play of sunshine and quickly moving cloud shadows give life and beauty to the whole scene in a way that is hardly possible in the more varied country (Illus. 6).

A large part of the fells into which the dales are cut has been rough pasture from the time when the prehistoric forest cover was first attacked and clearances were made by Bronze Age or even Neolithic settlers. It has experienced long periods of more or less continuous grazing and the sheep have prevented forest growth, but, except for the small fields of Brigantian farms of the Iron Age and Romano-British times, its turf has remained unbroken. Because of this the limestone areas of well-drained grassland are now a rich museum of earthwork from prehistoric and medieval times. Isolated hut foundations and small crofts from the Late Bronze Age merge into those of the Iron Age and Romano-British times. From the centuries of the Roman settlement there are many native villages with their fields, some remaining Celtic in all their features, but some showing the effect of Roman contacts. Superimposed on this older pattern there are foundations of Norse shepherds' houses of the tenth to thirteenth centuries, overlapping with the three and a half centuries when much of the limestone pasture was monastic sheep walk. There are boundary banks, ditches, sheep houses, folds and green trackways linked with monastic granges, all contributing their quota to the rich palimpsest on the more open ground along the terraces of each dale. On the highest ground and over most of the Millstone Grit tops, there is heather moor or a thick peat cover with cotton grass and boggy ground on which little trace of early activity can be found.

One of the remarkable aspects of the dales country is the sense of unity of the area along with a strong individual character to each dale. The underlying unity is never lost although the briefest examination will tell one who knows the dales, by countless small details, exactly which one he is in.

The geological differences already outlined naturally affect the physical shape of the dales, so that Ribblesdale and Wharfedale are dominated by the massive crags of the Great Scar Limestone. In Wensleydale the repeated limestones of the Yoredales form long scars and terraces along the valley sides and the fellsides go up in large steps over each limestone. Below Askrigg the valley opens out to a great width and the sense of being in a dale is almost lost (Illus. 7). Swaledale keeps a very narrow form, gorge-like in parts, even as far as Richmond, and in this is more akin to Nidderdale, which also is a narrow valley. The western dales which come together near Sedbergh are shorter, generally steeper-sided and in their lower part near Sedbergh are cut in the precarboniferous slates. They make a form different from that of the limestone dales and more akin to the Lake District. This gives the north-west a special character, although without destroying the general character of the dales country.

Although most people do not regard the dales as an industrial area, past industries have to some extent left their mark on the countryside and particularly the villages have been affected by the growth and additions which are attributable to the industries. In the seventeenth, eighteenth and nineteenth centuries several industries flourished for a time, then disappeared, but their remains have become a part of the scene, just as the twentieth-century usage of the dales is contributing something of slight change. Perhaps the easiest and clearest way to deal with this aspect of the dales is to look briefly at their social and economic history and at what is now called industrial archaeology, as a background to the detailed studies which make up the bulk of this book.

In all the dales which run to the Vale of York there is a point where the character of the dale changes, above which the villages with a centre, with well-spread fields and with one or two larger houses, characteristic of the lower dale, are replaced by what can only be called small hamlets, only a cluster of a few cottages with no particular plan and few fields. This change occurs at the line marking what was the edge of the pre-Norman and medieval forests. In Swaledale at Reeth, Wensleydale at Askrigg, Nidderdale at Pateley Bridge and Wharfedale at Kettlewell, this change occurs. To the west of these villages the country was 'forest' in the legal sense with its keepers, foresters and all the officials of the forest courts. Settlement was restricted, agriculture was almost impossible and only a very sparse population could find a living. The basic settlement of these forest parts was that of the Norse sheep farmers of the tenth century, whose farms were taken over and converted to forest lodges. These Norse farms retained their names and we now have such hamlets as Yockenthwaite, Burtersett, Appersett, Countersett, Ramsgill, Muker, Gunnerside, and individual farms like Winterscales, Knudmaning, Fossdale, Lofthouse, Bouthwaite and so on, in great number. Garsdale, Dentdale and the Rawthey valley are all typical of forest settlement, with only one large village, Sedbergh, now a small market town – though the market has almost disappeared – at the junction of the three valleys.

This forest edge marks very nearly the limit of the Anglo-Danish penetration from the east which gave us our present villages with their recognizable plans built round a village green or a long street, the crofts behind each house and the town fields embracing the whole, with outlying 'common pastures' and the moor. A rough distinction, of greater significance in the Middle Ages, was that west of this forest line there was little or no agriculture, east of it the basis was arable cultivation of common fields. Today, the distinction has nearly gone, except that sheep dominate in the west and stock-raising and dairying in the east.

From this generalization we can turn to the individual dales. Swaledale, from the river source down to Richmond where it

opens out into the plain, is about thirty miles long, with Grinton, nine miles above Richmond, providing the parish church
of all the upper dale. Across the river from Grinton is Reeth,
the market town of the dale. The valley, from a few miles
below Grinton to within three miles of its head, is dominated
by the lead-mining industry. The records of mining start in
the twelfth century, but there is sufficient evidence to suggest a
longer history than this. It continued into the opening years of
this century, but the great decline was in the second half of the
nineteenth century. The commonest feature on the fells on
each side of the Swale is the spoil heap of a mine, and every gill
has level mouths, washing floors, hushes and other traces of
mine activity. Hushes are deep channels cut down the hillsides
by artificial torrents of water used by the miners to strip off the
soil and expose rock. This is a very old method of prospecting,
and such hushes are abundant and attract a great deal of attention and speculation from the visitor. Smelt mills, now all
ruined, are in evidence, more than twenty having been active
at one time or another. When the industry was near its greatest
prosperity, about the 1830s, there were over 850 lead miners in
a total population of just under 7,000, about one in eight of the
total population, men, women and children, while farmers and
their labourers numbered about 270. There had been a big
influx into the dale about the end of the eighteenth century and
this led to the building of tiny cottages in the existing villages,
so that there is a recognizable pattern in these rather crowded
mining villages updale from Reeth (Illus. 9). The depressions
of the early nineteenth century forced many families out of
mining and there was great migration, some going into the
coalfields of the east, many into the textile towns of Lancashire.
This left, as a feature of the mining villages, many deserted
cottages and hovels which only recently have been rescued, two
or even three being combined as one and restored and improved as weekend or retirement houses. The agriculture is
confined to sheep-breeding and rearing and a little stock and
dairy farming.

Wensleydale has some lead mines, but these are nothing like
so numerous or visible as those in Swaledale, and nowhere do

they make an important feature; nor did they affect the population movements in the same way. Near the head of the dale and again near Carperby there has been in the past a fairly large quarrying industry, mainly roofing slates and flagstones, and around the dale head there was in the nineteenth century a large number of small collieries working coals in the Yoredale Series. The most significant aspect of Wensleydale is the richness of its farms below Askrigg and the number of its large estates with their fine houses. The great breadth of dale has made room for large halls like Bolton, Danby, Burton and others with room for large parks, and there are the castles of Bolton and Middleham. In this rich farming country it is a little unexpected to come across a large mill like that at Aysgarth or the groups at Askrigg, at Hawes and Gayle, all at one time employed in the worsted spinning trade (see Chapter Six). The decline in population, present in common with all our rural areas, is proportionately far less than in Swaledale. The very small amount of mining and the extent of the richer farming acted as a buffer against sudden variations, so that family migrations are far less a part of the Wensleydale story than in other dales. The growth of the cheese industry, first in almost every farmhouse, then later on a factory scale at Hawes, Aysgarth and Thoralby provided occupation for women which compensated in part for the closing of the textile mills. Livestock markets at Leyburn and Hawes and the presence of the railway from Northallerton through the length of the dale to Garsdale Junction encouraged dairying and gave an outlet for milk and other produce direct to London or other large towns (Illus. 8). Of all the dales Wensleydale has been the most prosperous and this is reflected in the style and size of the houses and the general appearance of its villages.

To some frequenters of the dales Nidderdale may appear to be rather out of the way. It owes this feeling largely to the absence of a through road to and beyond the valley head; the main road is the one from Ripon and Harrogate which merely intersects and crosses the dale at Pateley Bridge. Nidderdale, for a great part of its history, was a portion of the huge parish of Kirkby Malzeard away on the eastern edge of our area, and its orientation has been that way rather than into the other dales. Monastic connexions of the dale were with Fountains and Byland abbeys, both to the east, and much of its land was in the Forest of Knaresborough.

At the end of the eighteenth century it was reported as being a great producer of butter and bacon on a large number of small farms, and these were sent respectively to London and east Lancashire. Its connexion with Knaresborough is emphasized by its development of a flax and hemp industry for which several mills were built around Pateley Bridge. The ruins of many of these mills, all driven by water-wheels, are still to be found on the side streams of the valley. Since 1893 Bradford Corporation has invaded the valley for its water supply and has built three reservoirs, Gouthwaite 1900, Angram 1904 and Scar House 1936. Leeds has the neighbouring valley of the Washburn, a tributary of the Wharfe, and the last of their three reservoirs, Thruscross, only filled this year, 1967, has drowned a fine group of flax mills and their associated housing, for many years ruined and known as the 'deserted village'.

Wharfedale is perhaps more associated in the popular mind with visitors than are the other dales because of the presence in it of Ilkley and Bolton Abbey. Ilkley, a few miles outside our boundary, has for a long time been the 'gateway' to Wharfedale. When its medicinal springs were rediscovered (for they had been used by the Romans) in the mid-nineteenth century, Ilkley became a spa, many large hydros were built and it became a resort of fashion. It remains a town with every facility for the visitor, an inland holiday resort alive to all its assets, attracting increasing numbers of visitors and residents to the dales. A few miles up the dale is Bolton Priory, a former house of Augustinian canons, set in a truly romantic position on the river bank, with miles of woodland paths open to the public. These beauties attracted Turner and Girtin, Gray and Wordsworth among many others, and they were visited by all Ilkley tourists. Above Bolton, Wharfedale offers miles of good walking, and good roads throughout its length for post-chaise and later wagonette parties made it known as 'visitors' country' (see Chapter Twelve). In 1902 the railway from Skipton to Grassington brought the dale into easy access from the Lancashire and Yorkshire industrial towns.

The great lead-mining industry which was so important from the seventeenth century up to about 1880 was located on the moors along the north side of the valley and nowhere intruded into the visible scene of the valley itself. Thus Wharfedale has always appeared as a fine farming area with a few textile mills particularly round Grassington and Hebden, although both mining and textiles have played a large part in the population movements in the past (see Chapter Eleven). When the textile industry left the dale, its place was taken by limestone quarrying and burning which is concentrated in Linton, Threshfield and Kilnsey.

That portion of Airedale which comes within the dales area is only the five miles at the head of the dale leading to Malham and Malham Moor, and the popularity of Malham is now such that few people think of this part of the dale except as the road to Malham. The popularity of Malham is phenomenal and has reached proportions which are setting very difficult problems for the area. Motor coaches, up to twenty or more, are seen in the village daily during the week, and at holidays forty or more are a common sight. Cars crowd every inch of the place, and people swarm in their hundreds. In an average week in the summer terms up to 600 or 700 schoolchildren may be brought to Malham, and the strain on the biological reserves of flora and fauna is near breaking-point. The reason for this enormous popularity is not obvious – it is a growth of the twentieth century starting with the bicycle and getting out of hand with the motor-car.

The Pennine Way traverses Airedale by the riverside, then climbs across Malham Moor and by way of Fountains Fell and Penygent links it with Ribblesdale. The ten miles of dale between Settle and Ribblehead are flanked by the magnificent mountains of Ingleborough and Penygent and it is largely on those that the attention focuses. The dale is dependent, as all are, on stock and sheep farming, but the largest employment is found in the big quarries near Settle, around Helwith Bridge three miles up from Settle, again at Horton in Ribblesdale and also at Ribblehead. These are all large-scale mechanized modern quarries and the output of roadstone and lime from the dale adds up to something much more than a million tons a year. Ribblesdale is, however, the approach to a wonderland of caves and potholes on the flanks of Ingleborough and Penygent and around Ribblehead, and every weekend one meets bands of hardy youths festooned with ropes and rope ladders, camping gear and other apparatus, setting out for one of the most strenuous of all the outdoor sports of this area.

On the western side of Ingleborough there are small dales surrounding Whernside, across which the potholing country extends. Running down from the high country around Ribblehead, Widdale descends to Wensleydale and Dentdale carries one to Sedbergh. The small dales in the north-west corner, Dentdale, Garsdale and the Rawthey, are gems in their own right. Narrow, peaceful and hiding beautiful waterfalls, amazing river scenery and a wealth of attractive seventeenth- and eighteenth-century houses in their whole length, they are becoming more and more rewarding to those who explore them. In Dentdale the traces of the old Dent marble industry are still met with in the many gills and on the moor edge, but otherwise the picture is one of scattered Norse-type farms, on some of which the sledge is still used in preference to the horse-drawn cart for carrying the hay on these very steep slopes, and milk is brought in from the outlying shippons in the back can. It is a country in marked contrast with the rest of the dales, but still it is an integral part of them and cannot be mistaken for any other country than the Yorkshire dales.

CHAPTER TWO

Discovering a village

THE VILLAGE of Rilston, or Rylstone, lies about halfway between Skipton and Grassington on the modern road, as it lay on the old one which still winds as a green lane for most of its way along the foot of the fells a little to the east of the present road. It is on the watershed between the Aire and the Wharfe, four miles from Skipton and five miles from Grassington. About half a mile to the east the ground rises steeply to the gritstone edge of Rilston Fell 700 ft above and 1,500 ft above sea level, and to the west it rises more gently to the heights of Malham Moor.

The church stands on a slight hill at the edge of the village, and a number of houses cluster round an artificial pond which last century replaced the green. Many of the houses in Rilston, however, are hidden from the road, scattered among crofts which have sufficient trees to hide them. The history of the village has little place in published sources and, apart from references to the Nortons once associated with it, it is almost ignored, finding place neither in Wharfedale nor Airedale topographies. How does one set about discovering the story of such a village? How much of its history can be recovered? The manor rolls and other records have not been found, few manorial surveys are known, all we have are a few deeds and conveyances of land in the seventeenth and eighteenth centuries, the enclosure award of 1772 and the tithe award of the mid-nineteenth century. However, one great asset hitherto totally ignored is the land itself, and a detailed survey of this, acre by acre, reveals abundant evidence of the past history. This survey was undertaken by a small group of students from a university tutorial class on local studies and field archaeology, working with their tutor. Let us see if we can trace these discoveries in the field and see what interpretation can be placed upon them.

The first aspect of Rilston township to be looked at was its boundaries. The township, or civil parish, is narrow and elongated, measuring five miles from north to south; for more than half its length from the north it is not more than a mile or even, in parts, half a mile wide. At the foot of this long neck the township expands to the east forming a 'foot' very like the foot of a stocking, three miles at its greatest length west to east, and about a mile wide north to south (Fig 3). This is a most unusual shape for a township in this part of the Pennines, but is nearly matched by the neighbouring Hetton. On walking the boundary and using the map, the first characteristic to catch the attention is the fact that only a part of the total length is formed by any natural feature, and that the slight watersheds of the area lie in the main within the township and not along its boundaries – the township straddles across and along a watershed. If one starts in the south-east corner, the boundary which is between Rilston and Barden comes to a point in the middle of the Upper Barden Reservoir, where Yethersgill and a tributary stream join. Up Yethersgill, at a great stone known as Grey Mare in Yethersgill, Thorpe, Burnsall, Cracoe and Rilston boundaries meet in a point. We are here in the midst of a wild heather moor, and at 1,350 ft OD. After the common boundary with Cracoe, the boundary is between Rilston and Linton, then between Rilston and Threshfield. The north end of the township shares its boundary with Bordley, then much of its western line is common with Hetton, then with Winterburn and Flasby. To the south it shares its boundary with Stirton and Thoralby, then with Embsay and Eastby and so back to the point of origin. So the township has a common boundary with thirteen surrounding townships. How can such a state of affairs come about? We need to look at the wider pattern of the settlement of Airedale and Wharfedale before a reasonable explanation can be found.

When the first wave of Anglian settlers came into this part of west Yorkshire, probably after the fall of the Celtic kingdom of

Elmet in the early years of the seventh century, they settled in the long river valleys, often in the woodland in which they made clearings, giving to their settlements place names ending in -*leah* or as we now write it -*ley*, such as Ilkley, Drebley, Shipley and so on. Bordley is one of the few exceptions in which a -ley name is away from the river valley, but in the

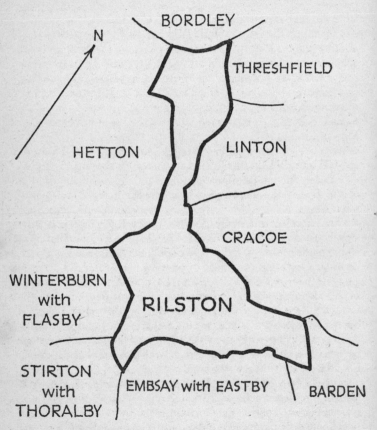

Fig 3. The boundaries of Rilston township

head of a small tributary. Other and slightly later settlers
moved beyond the densely wooded gritstone country of the
-*leys*, into the limestone country with its thinner cover of
scrub and more pasture, settling in small family farm groups
with the suffix -*tun* now -*ton*, like Skipton, Grassington, Linton
and so on. These early villages were almost all along the river
bank, with their land, which became the township, stretching
up from the riverside towards the watershed, making a long,
roughly parallel-sided township usually about three miles along
the river but possibly three, four or more miles up to the watershed. They had a regular zoned arrangement, meadowland
along the river alluvium, arable land on the foot slopes, then
common pasture, and above that, on the high ground, the
waste. Where valleys were wide the hunger for land was sometimes satisfied before the watershed was reached. So it happened that there were areas of no-man's-land left here and
there, sometimes merely a ridge-top but sometimes, on the
lower watersheds, a wide-spreading area of small streams and
shallow valleys, a rather featureless expanse. In such an un-
claimed area an individualist, or maybe an overspill generation
from a crowded neighbouring village, might seek to start a new
settlement with room and opportunity to develop their own
land. This overspill was helped by the custom of dividing
inheritance between all the sons of a family, so that in a few
generations a holding might be far too small to support a man
and his family and new ground had to be found. It seems likely
that a number of these overspill townships were formed in the
eighth and ninth centuries. Here we have the most probable
explanation of the founding of Rilston as also of Hetton and
Bordley, almost the last pieces to be fitted into the jigsaw puzzle
of the township pattern. Rilston, which straddles along the
watershed and neighbours in between thirteen other townships,
must have had this sort of very late occupation.[1]

But what of Ril, or Hroll the Shiverer, the Norseman who
gave his name to Rils-ton? The land had been apportioned in
the valleys, but it was not the end of invasions. First after the
Angles came the Danes, who, having made peace with the
Angles, entered the district in small numbers as peaceful

settlers from A D 876 to about 900. They set up single farms or small hamlets, with names ending in *-by* and *-thorpe* respectively, in outlying parts of townships on land given to them by agreement with some Anglian village. So 'satellite' villages began and we now have Embsay with Eastby, Burnsall with Thorpe, Stirton with Thoralby and Winterburn with Flasby, all bordering on Rilston.

The Angles and Danes had all come from the east coast, but the last pre-Conquest immigrants came from the west coast over the hills. These were the Norsemen who, during the tenth and eleventh centuries, spread from Northern Ireland and came as sheep farmers, seeking the still unoccupied upland pastures which had no attraction for the Angles and Danes. Often they started single farm settlements, with names such as Scale and Bucross, the latter being originally Bu Cross, an Irish 'cross' name. Probably Scale (House) takes its name from such a settlement, and its position on a shelf of the hillside is very characteristic of many other 'scales', the shielings of cattle herders, many of which were formed in the hills of the west. As these Norsemen prospered they 'invaded' some of the Anglian villages and, though they took to village ways, they sometimes gave them new names, possibly on marrying the daughter of the headman. They were accustomed to giving personal names or to calling them after king and priest, and so we have Coniston (king's tun), Long Preston (priest's tun) and, in the same way, Rilston (the tun of Hroll the Shiverer).

Around Bucross at the northern extremity of the township there is a scatter of small farms within a few fields recovered from the rough moorland, with two miles of wild moorland intervening between them and the Rilston houses. The old name is remembered now and contracted as Bucker House, which is locally often pronounced Buckrus, very near to its original sound. Around it there are other houses: Lainger House, Park House and so on, and these preserve the Norse *-hus* or farm. Around Scale House there are again several fields separated from the town fields of Rilston by a wide belt of rougher pasture, and forming a little self-contained settlement which may have been separate through much of medieval time.

Such is the story which one can suggest for the earliest history of Rilston, but the Norsemen continued to spread even after the Conquest, possibly on into the thirteenth century, making a few new settlements in more remote parts and occasionally filling in unoccupied spaces between the older ones. One of these late settlements was Cracoe, which adjoins Rilston, and another was Skirethorns, within the bounds of Threshfield. Cracoe is not named in the Domesday Survey, and like Rilston it has no land going down to any of the rivers, but straddles the watershed between Aire and Wharfe, and seems to fill in an irregular gap between more normal Anglian townships and Rilston.

At the time of the Norman Conquest Rilston was a township in which there were two manors held in the time of Edward the Confessor by Almunt, who had 4 carucates and Ravenchil who had 1½ carucates. Almunt's manor was granted to Dolfin but Ravenchil the Norseman kept possession of his. In this area the carucate appears to have been about 80 acres, so Ravenchil and his tenants had about 120 acres which remained separate from the rest of the township, the other manor becoming part of the Honour of Skipton. As late as the end of the eighteenth century the occupants of Bucross and Scale House were independent freeholders who owned both soil and minerals. While the manor of Rilston passed through several medieval and later ownerships and became part of the Clifford fee, Bucross and Scale remained isolated and retained many of their Norse features.

Today the village has no 'green', only a pond and a large area of crofts around which the houses are ranged with farm buildings among them, forming an approximate square which represents the earlier open area of the green; in fact, the group of houses on the south side are still called, as a group, Rilston Green. There is a small group outside this pattern: the church, the farm which has replaced the old hall and one or two other houses, clustered on a slight hill on the edge of the village. On all sides there are fields, some are meadow but most are pasture, the farms being almost entirely occupied in dairy farming and stock-rearing, with a few sheep as supplement. In the majority of the fields a pattern of ridges can be seen, some very plainly visible at all times, others seen only in a favourable light. Close examination revealed that the ridges were in related groups of a dozen or more parallel riggs, with slight furrows between them, and that many of these showed a curvature in the shape of a reversed S, though the curvature was only small. This is the true characteristic mark of medieval 'rigg and furrow' plough-ing, and it suggests that if all the rigg and furrow could be sur-veyed accurately we would have a map which would include the medieval town fields and would be able to decide the extent of the ploughlands. Some riggs, however, were found to be straight and rather narrow and all these seemed to lie mainly nearer the outskirts of the village. As a few conveyances of 'land newly enclosed' referred in each case to fields with these straight riggs, it appeared that they marked the sixteenth- and seventeenth-century expansion of the older town fields.

The separate groups of rigg and furrow in which the riggs lie parallel to each other and which are the 'furlongs' of the old fields, often having their own name, varied in size from about 5 to 25 acres, but most of the groups approximated to 10 acres. The furlongs are seen to be in four distinct groupings, the boundaries of which are either the older roads or prominent boundary ditches and balks or banks. Three of these large groups can be recognized as the ancient arable fields of the village, and across the middle of each there is a way, now pre-served as a narrow lane or marked out by low banks between the adjacent furlongs. These are the access roads into the com-mon fields and all the furlongs can be reached from them. One of them, much wider than the others, is the 'outgang', the broad way through the fields by which the cattle could be driven to and from the common pastures which lay outside.

The fourth group of furlongs are the later ones added as 'in-takes' in the sixteenth and seventeenth centuries, but these are mostly marked by a rigg and furrow which is straight and never curved and generally narrower and shallower than the earlier form. The map (Fig 4) shows the result of this investigation and is, in fact, a plan of medieval and later fields recovering, en-tirely by mapping what can still be seen on the ground.

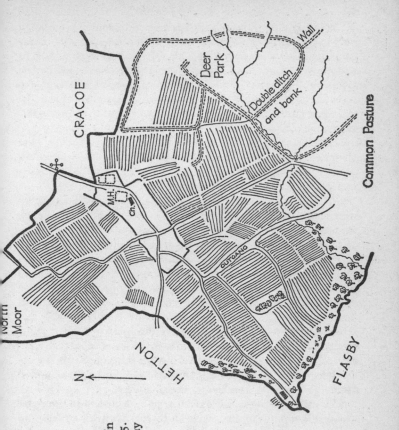

Fig 4. Rig and furrow in Rilston, surveyed in 1965. New road and railway omitted

We see Rilston then, say in the fifteenth century, as a village with three arable fields which for convenience we call South Field, East Field and North Field, approximately 140, 120 and 120 acres respectively. Fields between the South Field and the township boundary, Calton Gill Beck, were added in the seventeenth century as Mill Gates, Low Field and Kellands, and those between South Field and Hetton Beck were ploughed some time after the enclosure of North Moor in 1772, of which they form a small part. It seems likeliest that these fields were ploughed during the Napoleonic Wars, early in the nineteenth century, when most of the older fields were well-established pasture or were in hay.

Besides the compact fields just described, two other areas were found at the extreme south and north boundaries of the township. At the north end a few fields around the old houses of Lane Head and Bucker House are marked by riggs and furrows, but of the late, straight and narrower type. This area is separated by Boss Moor Common from the North Moor which was enclosed by the Act of 1772, and is indeed the Norse settlement of Bucross, with only about 100 acres of enclosed land.

To the south of Rilston, Scale House has around it some 100 acres of fields with rigg and furrow, but is separated from the Rilston fields by a broad belt of very rough pasture, part of the Bark which in 1772 was enclosed as a part of the common stinted (regulated) pastures of the township.

The only document which can give us a clue to the population of Rilston in the time when these various fields were in full use is the poll tax returns of 1379.[2] The village then had a population of twenty-five men and thirty-one women, besides children under the age of sixteen. William de Rilston was lord of the manor; there were two weavers, one of them weaving shalloons, a light cloth for dresses, and the rest of the villagers were peasants. There was Robert Milner the miller, and there may have been a priest or chaplain at the manor house who would not be named in the tax roll. We do not know any details about William de Rilston, but things changed slowly and a record of his ancestor Elias, 100 years earlier, tells us that he held 70 acres of arable land and 21 acres of good meadow with 21 bovates of poorer land, a wood and a large garden. All the work on these demesne lands was done by the villeins, that is, the unfree tenants, though his three free tenants owed certain services agreed upon individually. In 1373 Peter Mauleverer, who had owned manorial lands in a part of the township, sold his lands in Rilston and with them sold the services of his free tenants and the actual persons of his villeins and their sequelae (ie, their wives and offspring) and chattels, just as though they were oxen or horses.

Of the fourteenth-century village buildings nothing now survives, but we know the sites they occupied. The cottages of the present village, mainly seventeenth-century buildings, fit into the pattern of the fields, with the field roads all converging on the present village centre; there is no trace of any other arrangement. The centre of the village was at the ford of which part of a paving was found during recent road alterations, where the old road coming north from Scale, between East and South Fields, continued, after crossing the stream, across North Field by the lane now called Mucky (ie, dirty) Lane. The old road was crossed in the village by the road from Hetton to the church and hall. In the road alterations near the ford and against the traces of the old hall gardens, a moderate quantity of pottery fragments was turned out, mainly fourteenth- and fifteenth-century ware. This road continued on to Cracoe and Grassington, and where it crossed the township boundary there is the base of a massive cross, set on a small mound at the side of the road. From the cross the boundary is continued across the fields by a ditch and bank on which are the remains of several very old thorn trees.

The church, though entirely rebuilt in 1853, preserves the traces of earlier buildings in a few fragments. Built into the vestry wall, inside, there is an arch head of Romanesque style, probably part of a window of the first church; there are also two very early capitals and the head of a stone cross which are of twelfth- or thirteenth-century date. The church has been rebuilt more than once and nothing else of the early work has survived. However, we know that in the twelfth century Symon presb: (presbiter) de Rilleston witnessed a deed of William de Rillestun who died in 1175. The status then would be that of a chapel attached to the hall, and, in fact, Rilston remained a chapel of ease in the parish of Burnsall until 1876, when it was separated and formed the parish of Rilston, serving Hetton and Cracoe as well.

From the bottom of the green a lane goes between South Field and the southern part of North Moor and is in part still called Mill Lane. Where the stream, Hetton Beck, leaves the township of Rilston a close search in thick brushwood and nettles uncovered the foundations of a small building with, at one end of it, a hollow recognizable as the site of the wheelpit. A further search revealed a fine watercourse more than 100 yards long, from the stream to the top of a structure which was high enough to allow a 25-ft wheel in the pit. Such a wheel, of course, was far larger than the early cornmill could have used and was obviously the wheel of the rebuilt and extended mill which in the early nineteenth century was a worsted mill. The early mill was mentioned in 1295 as the water-mill of Rilston and Hetton, and the road from the mill to Hetton can still be recognized in part in Hetton fields. The mill, a moiety of which in 1295 was valued at 53s 4d (£2.67), had increased in 1569 to £200 on a forty-year purchase and in 1605 it was leased to William Wallock for ninety-nine years at £3 a year. One of the mill services laid upon tenants of the manor was the provision of millstones and labour for the repair of the mill. In two places on Rilston Fell a finished and a partly finished millstone are still lying partly imbedded in the soil. It is clear in each case that they have been made from neighbouring large boulders of Millstone Grit, which have been split by using a row of wedges. On the many parts of boulders still lying about there is a row of half-wedge slots and it seems from this that the early millstones were taken from stone lying about and not quarried. However, there are some small quarries under the rocky edge of Rilston Fell where stone has been levered out and where areas of chippings mark an old dressing floor. There are some partly-dressed stones there against small benches of rock which were loading places. From the side of these benches a deeply worn sledge way goes down the hillside, and they join together with tracks from the millstone area. The rock from the quarries was used in the larger houses in the seventeenth- and eighteenth-century rebuilding.

The foundations of the old hall are now in part covered by a seventeenth-century farm and its outbuildings, but there is an enclosure in which the farm stands and which also includes the church and churchyard in its extent; within this there are many mounds and hollows over which drainage ditches and other excavations have turned out bits of pottery of thirteenth- to seventeenth-century date.

In 1881 a writer on Craven, Dixon, says of the old hall, 'not a stone remains' but

> towards the end of last century and even later portions of the ruined hall were still standing. The venerable mother of the late Francis King used to describe it as it then existed. She would tell of mullioned casements, of pointed arches, of square turrets, of capacious fire-places, and clustered chimneys . . . The building must have been erected as early as the reign of Henry VI.

It is more likely that the old hall as remembered with these features was built nearer the end of the fifteenth century when John Norton married Anne Radcliffe and so obtained the lordship of the manor of Rilston.[3] Whitaker, writing in 1811, said

> there are near the house (now in decay), large remains of a pleasure ground, such as were introduced in the early part of Elizabeth's time, with topiary works, fish-ponds, and island, etc.

The fishponds, with an island in one of them, are still there, though dry, alongside the old road, and the many mounds already described no doubt represent much of the pleasure grounds. The estates remained with the Nortons until the Rising of the North, when for his share in it Norton of Rilston forfeited all his estates. A survey of the forfeiture states that the demesne land was about 400 acres and that there were 43 tenements some with 2 oxgangs or bovates of land, some with only one or less and some only crofts. The land of the township was in open town fields. There were 130 red deer and some woodland which had been robbed of many trees, leaving 86 stumps of oak, 144 stumps of ash, 217 stumps of ellers, 99 stumps of hollies, the oaks valued at 1s (5p) each, the ash at 4d (1½p), ellers and hollies at a 1d (½p).

There had been trouble between the Nortons of Rilston and the Cliffords of Skipton, who hunted in the adjoining Crookrise Woods and accused the Nortons of tempting their deer into a small deer park or enclosure in Rilston. A large area of steep and rough fellside is called on some maps 'hall demesne' and an attempt to delimit it on the ground led to some interesting conclusions about the possible deer park or wood. At one point along the old road, towards Scale House, a double ditch can be seen running for a short way up the fellside. This was followed and found to be a high bank with a broad ditch on each side from which no doubt the bank had been built. Part way up the hill the ditch turned through ninety degrees to run north along the contour of the hillside, and from this corner the foundations of an ancient wall continue up the hill to the large rocky crags which form the Rilston Fell Edge. The ditch goes along the fellside, but because of the high growth of bracken and because the bank has deflected the hill drainage in parts and formed boggy areas it was not easy to follow. It dipped down into two deep stream gullies but climbed the opposite side, and a lot of careful search in winter, with every indication carefully mapped, soon showed the continuous line of the ditch. Near the north boundary of the township it turns westward down the hillside into the pastures and was traced across them nearly to the fishponds. This big ditch and the boundary bank of the town fields enclose approximately 125 acres in two subdivisions, one called Crutching Close, of 75 acres, and the other, which we like to think of as the deer park, of 50 acres. In addition, the old wall already mentioned, the foot of the crags along the edge, and another ditch from the north-west corner of Crutching Close enclose the hall demesne of about 150 acres. None of these ditches appear on any map and there seems to be no tradition of them among the present population.

In depositions taken by the President of the Council at York, at a meeting held between 1541 and 1560 (in the time of the first Norton lord of Rilston manor) when Lord Clifford was claiming the right to hunt deer out of Rilston, a boy said in evidence that he had seen keepers chase deer out of all parts of Rilston, and of Mr Norton he said, 'to draw in the Lord of Clifford's deer into his ground, he hath made a wall on an high rigge, beside a quagmire, and at the end of the wall he hath rayled the ground, so that it is a destruction to my Lord's deer so many as come'. Free warren had been granted to the lord of the manor of Rilston in 1258 and because of this Norton maintained his right to have and to hunt deer within Rilston manor and to treat the Cliffords as trespassers. His claim was upheld.

At the south end of the township, on a very prominent hill spur between Scale House and the fell, there stand the ruins of Norton Tower, visible as a landmark from a very wide area. From all points of view the ruin has a romantic and tantalizing appearance due to its shape and setting. Only the four corners remain, the central parts of the four walls having been pulled out when the tower was 'slighted' nearly 400 years ago. Below the ruins there is a steep wooded slope and on one side a deep rocky gill and noisy beck, Waterford Gill. Around and behind the tower there is the rough moorland pasture of the Bark leading up on to the wild moorlands of Barden Fell.

There is no precise date for the tower, but in the records of the College of Arms it is stated 'that Richard Norton, last of the Nortons, builded a tower in the farthest part of his lordship of Rilston, near Crookrise. He used to lie in summer always at his house at Rillestone, which his father or grandfather had by marriage of Radcliffe's daughter'. The family was Norton of Conyers, and seems to have spent only the summers at Rilston; if the tower was built for recreation, it was some time after 1500.

The nearly level summit of the hill promontory on which the tower stands is enclosed by a massive wall of which only parts remain here and there, and part of this wall is built on a broad bank with a ditch on the outer side. The bank and ditch were found to run all round the hill, enclosing the steep slopes as well as the top, and with a palisade of timber on the bank it would be a most efficient fence. The total area enclosed is about sixty acres. Within the flatter area on the hilltop there are several flat-topped mounds surrounded by ditches, which may have been rabbit warrens. There are also about thirty small cairns of stones obviously arranged to hold posts and these, although no regular pattern can be seen when mapped, may have been for jousting games or horsemanship. The tower is rectangular, 32 ft by 27 ft outside, with walls 4 ft thick. There are traces of a doorway on the south side and the first steps of a staircase in the south-east corner. The highest part of the walls is now only 15 ft.

Richard Norton, who built the tower, was a man of importance in the north of England, a member of the Council of the North and for some time Governor of Norham Castle, on Tweed. In 1567–8 he was High Sheriff of Yorkshire. His family was large, seven daughters and eleven sons, and no doubt when they were in residence in Rilston the village became a lively place. It would be for some of these sons that the tower was built, and they would have made the arrangements for games and sport. Richard took a share in the Rising of the North, with several of his sons, and for this he was exiled and died in Spanish Flanders, while two of his family, his brother Thomas and his son Christopher, were executed at Tyburn. Four of Norton's ordinary servants, from Rilston, were hanged near the village, and the estates were confiscated to the Crown. In 1600 an 'Extent . . . of Rilleston manor . . .' was made which showed that there were 47 tenements, most of them having land in the common fields 1, 2 or 3 bovates in extent and with rents varying from 2s (10p) to 18s (90p). The bovate, the land ploughed by one ox, varied between 12 and 15 acres in Rilston. The mill was in the hands of a tenant who paid £3 a year for it. This estate and manor was granted in 1605 to the Cliffords who very soon sold most of the tenements, which are still freehold, reserving only the manorial dues. Since that sale the manor has never had a resident lord.

The eighteenth century was a time of quiet development in which the arable land was almost entirely put down to grass and the enclosure of the open fields was accomplished by agreement. The few conveyances and deeds which remain show the frequent sale or exchange of strips and small pieces in the town fields from which new fields were created. The farming became mainly concerned with dairying and beef cattle with some breeding cattle. For a time the Boss Moor Fair was an event of importance at which great numbers of Scottish cattle were sold and at which local farmers bought stock to over-winter on their pasture (see Chapter Eight).

The common pastures, North Moor, Langhill, Bark and Garforth Close, 769 acres, were enclosed by the award of 1772 and these pastures carried many Scottish cattle as well as sheep, acclimatizing and feeding ready for the butchers' sales of the following year.

In 1839 the tithes were commuted and the tithe award gives the land of the township as having only 5 acres of arable, 2,095 acres of meadow and pasture, 101 acres of woodland and 849 acres of common. The dwellings listed are fourteen house and garden, or house, barn and croft, and ten cottages, thus being only half the size it was in 1600. The parish register reveals that the population was made up of farmers and labourers with a small number of craftsmen, the total population being, in 1841, 121.

For a short time in the opening years of the nineteenth century the mill had been used for cloth manufacture and a few of the smaller cottages in the village were occupied by mill workers, but before 1839 the mill had been closed and the tithe award only notices 'a mill site on Mill Brow, 10 perches'. For the last century the village has been a place of quiet farming, seeing little change beyond the making of the new road in 1853. This is the Cracoe to Skipton turnpike and it runs in a nearly straight line between Rilston and its southern boundary, leaving the old road one field distant to the east. Where the old and new road meet at the boundary, there is Sandy Beck Bar, the only tollhouse on the road, so placed as to keep an eye on the traveller who might be disposed to slip by on the old road.

In 1901 the Yorkshire Dales Railway was built from Skipton to Threshfield; this traversed the western side of the township, but its station was placed on the boundary between Rilston and Cracoe to serve both places. The line closed in 1930 except for two goods trains a day and the traffic in coal and lime with the big limestone quarries at Swinden. Its place was taken by the bus service; the buses come right through the centre of the village and have given it an hourly link with Skipton. The vastly increased motor traffic of the last few years along the main road passes the head of the village without stopping and so the village retains much of its old charm and shows little sign of change. Its abundant trees, the dignified old houses and the pond give it an attractive appearance that we would hate to see altered.

CHAPTER THREE

Trust Lords of the manor

THERE IS a feature of village government in this part of the Pennines which often puzzles strangers from more uniform and conformist parts of the country. This is the fact that some of our villages are governed by a group of three or four individuals known as Trust Lords, Wise Men, or some other such name, or by a meeting of all the freeholders of the township, these various groups exercising all the functions and powers of lords of the manor. It is they to whom the royalties from mines and quarries are paid; they who regulate the use of the common pastures and decide upon the 'stint', the number of grazing animals to be allowed on the pastures each year. They do in fact act as, and are in all ways, the lord of the manor, holding the lordship in trust for the whole body of freeholders. Nearly every group of Trust Lords has its own peculiar constitution and nearly all stem from a late sixteenth- or early seventeenth-century date.

Of the many such villages or manors, Garsdale and Dent in the north-west of the county, Bainbridge and Woodhall in Wensleydale, Kettlewell, Conistone and Hebden in Wharfedale, are a few examples only, and two of them, Kettlewell and Conistone, both well documented, will serve to illustrate two ways in which these trusts arose. In seeking the origins two events come prominently into almost all cases, the Dissolution of the Monasteries and the Rising of the North. The monastic orders received enormous grants of lands and manors in the Pennines, where they became important sheep farmers and where, by common agreement gradually worked out, the different monastic communities tended to secure grants in particular areas so that they could build up a consolidated estate, easily managed from one or two granges. Thus, Furness Abbey secured a large area in upper Ribblesdale which included several contiguous townships; Fountains Abbey secured most of Littondale, all Malham Moor, all Bordley and much of Malham; and in similar fashion other houses observed what one might almost call their own 'spheres of influence', where the grants of lands and manors made a continuous area with few possessions of other monastic houses or persons making more than small islands within their bounds. At the Dissolution these lands were returned to the Crown and, through the Augmentations Office, many of them were in time sold as large areas, either to local lords, as much of the Littondale land was sold to the Cliffords of Skipton, and the Bolton Priory estates to the Earl of Cumberland, or to local families, often holders of lay positions under the monasteries. In this group an example is the Lambert family which secured much of the land in Malhamdale and the Proctors who got lands in Bordley.

The Rising of the North in 1569 led at its defeat to the sequestration of the lands of many of the leaders like the Earl of Westmorland, who as one of the Neville family had the Honour of Middleham which covered much of Wensleydale, and the Nortons who had several manors in Wharfedale and in other parts of the dales. In this way other estates which had been in lay hands went to the Crown. Some estates were sold to London merchants who were ready during the reign of Elizabeth I to speculate in land and many of these, of whom Sir Thomas Gresham is an example, soon resold parts of the monastic estates either to local gentry or to those tenants who could afford to purchase. Many estates and manors, however, remained in the hands of the Crown and, being so far away from any central control, were many of them subject to inefficient management, dishonest agents and local disputes and quarrels.

Matters came to a head during the early Stuart period, when James I and then Charles I were faced with a serious lack of finance when they both wished and needed to redevelop the Navy. Although the sale of Crown lands could by no means solve the financial problem, or even be regarded as a major contribution, nevertheless it was a source of ready cash and the

citizen merchants of London were in the main willing customers. Some of the northern manors were sold in these circumstances to a group of London citizens who, after estimate and
experience of the real value of the property and income to be
derived from it, resold either to an individual or to a group,
generally on trust for all the tenants of the manor. Kettlewell is
a good example of this kind of sale, so we might look at this
township in sufficient detail to see how the sales were accomplished and how the life of the township was affected (Illus. 11).

At the Norman Conquest Kettlewell manor was small, only
of one carucate extent in 1087, but it seems to have flourished
and expanded under the lordship of the de Arches family to
whom it was granted by the Percies, being part of their fee, as
it had grown to eight carucates by the end of the thirteenth
century. It descended through a daughter of the de Arches to
the Fauconberg family and to two brothers, Walter and Percy,
who in 1293 divided the manor between them in two equal
moieties. One moiety was granted almost at once to Coverham
Abbey along with half the advowson of the church and half of
the manor cornmill. The other moiety of manor, church and
mill descended through the families of Gray of Rotherfield and
the Deincourts and then by purchase of grant to Ralph Neville,
Earl of Westmorland. About the middle of the fourteenth
century the advowson of the church was reunited, but in all
other ways the two moieties continued for all practical purposes
as two separate manors. The thirteenth-century market charter
was granted in the Gray moiety.

The two moieties were united in the hands of the Crown by
the dissolution of Coverham Abbey in 1536 and the sequestra-
tion of the Neville estates on the attainder of the Earl of
Westmorland as a leader of the unfortunate Rising of the
North in 1569. The Neville estates were part of the Honours of
Middleham and Richmond, and in 1605, in preparation for their
sale, a survey was ordered. It is entitled 'A Survey of the
Lordships of Middleham and Richmond in the County of
Yorke, with theyre severall Parts and Divisions taken the Third
Yeare of King James by Thomas Johnson and Aaron Rath-
borne, Anno 1605'.[1] In this survey each tenant is named, then

follow in order the following items of information – how much
of any lease still has to run; what houses, outhouses and land
they held; what fines they had paid in the previous twenty
years; what yearly rent they paid to the King; the yearly value;
and the clear yearly improvement. From this survey we learn
that at Kettlewell the portion belonging to the Honour of
Middleham had

53 tenants; 41 houses; 81 outhouses; 578 acres 1 rood of
Meadow and Arable land; 370 Pasture gates; fynes paid in
20 years £56.16.2; yearly rent £19.6.2; yearly value £122.9.7.
The Cleare Improvement £103.3.5.

Mr. Emanuel Scroope holdeth the same (Scale Park) and
certayne gates in Carnie at the rent of £17.6.8. Demesne.
The Parke contaynes in quantity 600 acres; Pasture gates 16.
It is yearly worth £61.12.0. The Improvement £44.5.4.

The Bailife & forester of Kettlewell & Collector of the
rents there, for wch he hath ye occupacion of a peece of
ground called Berkenthwait & a horse gate in Scale Park & a
fee of £1.10.4. Markets. There are three Market Towns,
Middleham and Kettlewell within the Lop. of Middleham
and Richmond within that Lordship. Churches. Kettlewell
an Impropriation in the guift of Bernard Calvert.

In 1628

King Charles in the fourth yeare of his reigne to Edward
Ditchfield John Highlord Humphrey Clarke late Citizens of
London and Francis Mosse Citizen and Scrivenor of London
and their heirs conveyed all the manor of Kettlewell And by
the said Humphrey Clarke in his life tyme and Francis
Mosse after the death of the said Edward Ditchfield and
John Highlord in pursuance of several Acts of Common
Council

of the Mayor, Aldermen and Commoners of the City of London, conveyed the same to John Stone, Nathaniell Manton,
Methuselah Turner and Thomas Benson, citizens of London.

They by Indenture dated November 20th, 1656, conveyed and sold to Matthew Hewitt of Linton, Clerk, William Faucet, Thomas Ripley, John Bolland, Thomas Coats, James Bolland, John Ibbottson the elder, and Edmund Tennant of Kettlewell, yeomen, all the lordship or reputed lordship of Kettlewell with all messuages, cottages, arable land, pasture meadow, woods, etc, under diverse yearly rents amounting in the whole to £17 13s 7d (£17.68). This group, then, at various times, sold the tenements, houses and cottages with a proportion of land according to their ancient rent, but reserved all the royalties and liberties of fishing, fowling, hunting and hawking, of mines of coal and of lead and whatever else is appurtenant to the lordship of the manor, to be held in trust by them for the freeholders of the manor.

After the death of Matthew Hewitt and others, leaving Thomas Coats and John Ibbottson the only survivors, Coats and Ibbottson were desirous of establishing the trust left with them in the proper manner. From this and later discussions, the group known as the Trust Lords of Kettlewell were to be appointed by election of all the freeholders, to be not more than nine and not less than seven.

They then conveyed all the manor royalties and property to such persons as the freeholders of Kettlewell elected to succeed them and that procedure had been followed ever since whenever the trustees, by death, had been reduced to two or three. In 1883, when the trustees were reduced to four, a new group of eight were appointed, of whom five were landowners in Kettlewell but not living on their property. They agreed in a trust deed

to fix and establish for the future the trust and guardianship of the manor or lordship of Kettlewell to and for such uses as were at the time of purchasing the same intended for the benefit of the real owners and proprietors.

It was stated that the intention was that

all and every person then or at any time thereafter holding

any messuage, land etc. within the manor of Kettlewell . . .
should have annually from the date thereof in proportion to
his or her share of the rents issues and profits of the said
manor.

The proportion was that of the ancient rent which they paid for
their property of the total ancient rent of £17 13s 7d (£17.68).

New trustees were appointed, this time all of them freeholders living within the manor, and they were charged to
convene a meeting on the request of a majority of them, to hold
courts of the manor (Court Leet) to arrange for the appointment of new trustees when they were reduced to three, to
appoint a steward of the courts and a barmaster to grant ground
and to collect the royalties on lead and coal mines, a gamekeeper and a shepherd. This agreement has been followed
carefully ever since.[2]

The Trust Lords appointed a shepherd at an early date, and
the accounts kept by the bylawmen chosen to oversee the use
of the commons and pastures are extant from June 1777.[3] An
annual meeting was called to let the hirding (appoint the
shepherd for a year) and to decide the stint. The stint is the
number of sheep and/or cattle to be allowed to graze on common pastures and the dates between which the grazing
could take place. At a meeting, April 27th, 1848, for instance
'for letting the Hirding of Whernside and Top Mere (part of
the out moors) we order and agree that on Whernside one ewe
and lamb to go on one gate till the 9th of July and after that all
lambs are counted two to a gate'. Sheep gates and cattle or
beast gates are the essence of dales farming, the gate being the
right to graze the common pasture by a 'made' or full-grown
beast in the case of a beast gate, or by a full-grown sheep, on the
sheep gate. The matter of how many sheep are the equivalent
of one beast is usually settled at five, but the treatment of
lambs and calves is subject to special agreements.

The trustees also regulated the cutting of peat, a right of 'turbary' which all the freeholders possessed, the right to cut
bedding, usually bracken, for their cattle sheds, and the duty of
freeholders and gateholders to assist in draining and improving

the moors. The trustees could fine those who failed in these duties. The shepherd was to attend on the moor from the beginning of May to the end of October, was not to train young dogs on the moor, and was to repair walls and fill in dangerous bog holes. His wages were adjusted to the income which was got by the charge which all gateholders paid. In 1890 this was $5\frac{1}{2}d$ (2p) per gate levied on 1,019 gates, amounting to £23 7s $0\frac{1}{2}d$ (£23.35). With a small balance from the previous year, the total was divided out to 16s 6d ($82\frac{1}{2}$p) per week for thirty weeks, £24 15s (£24.75). The wages fluctuated between 9s 6d ($47\frac{1}{2}$p) in 1850 and £1 3s (£1.15) in 1875, then decreased to 16s 6d ($82\frac{1}{2}$p) in 1890. The number of gates increased to 1,178 in 1890. Each year's account gives a complete list of the gate-holders and thus becomes an important source of information on the village.

By 1800 the common pastures had become overstocked and not easy to manage, so an Enclosure Act was promoted by a number of the Trust Lords and freeholders for the common pastures and for a number of small parcels of land still remaining unenclosed among the open fields. This Act was granted and an award made by which the common pastures of Kettlewell Cam, Middlesmoor and Langliff were enclosed and stinted. This award was made jointly with Conistone and will be studied in more detail with that manor.

Soon after purchasing the manor the Trust Lords were faced with the leasing of their lead mines which had worked sporadically for many years. Within the manor boundaries there are three areas in which veins of lead ore are found, the head of Dowber Gill on Whernside Pasture, on the Cam Pasture and on Middlesmoor Pasture. The oldest traces of mining are on the groups of veins eventually worked near Dowber Gill. The right to work the mines of Kettlewell had been granted by the Crown at a date soon after its acquisition of the manor, in a comprehensive grant of the Honour of Middleham, the 1605 survey saying 'the mynes are taken of the King since the Cities contract, by Humphrey Wharton, receyvor here'. By a lease of September 30th, 1663, Matthew Hewitt and the other recently-appointed Trust Lords granted the mines within the manor of Kettlewell to Francis Smithson of Richmond, merchant. In March 1669, however, the un-expired term of this lease was surrendered for a new lease to Francis Smithson and his cousin, Philip Swale, who was agent for Lord Wharton in his Swaledale mines. This lease was of all the mines or veins of lead ore already opened on the moors, wastes and commons of Kettlewell, and liberty to search, dig, sink shafts, etc, there 'together with the Smelting Mylne near Kettlewell with the wheel, bellows, hearth and kiln holes for drying chopwood, and all other utensils belonging to the same'. The lessees were to give the Trust Lords a thirteenth part of all the ore got, or the fourth piece or fodder (2,464 lb.) of lead smelted, the trustees paying all the costs of smelting. In a deed of partnership of the next day, by which Smithson and Swale brought a Derbyshire miner, Barker, into a partnership with them, they recite an important clause, that the townsmen of Kettlewell are still to be allowed to work for lead ore within the manor as they had done in the past.[4]

Smithson, Swale and Barker worked these mines for many years, but production was never very great. Other mines opened on the Cam but again only in a modest way. The smelt mill, however, found work by smelting ores from the mines in some of the neighbouring townships and brought a small return to the freeholders. It became dilapidated in the depression of the second half of the eighteenth century and, in 1833, complaints of the destruction of pasture by fumes from the mill, and of harm done to cattle by poisoning, were con-sidered by the Court Leet and the Trust Lords decided to build a flue and chimney 'to take off the noxious fumes . . . and that the expenses be defrayed by the Trust Lords'. In 1859 one of the Trust Lords brought up the very unsatisfactory state of the mill, because of which some miners requested that they be allowed to pay their dues in ore and others asked to build their own mill. It was stated that two or three energetic companies were a principal source of income and employment in the township, and so the mines must be encouraged. It was not until 1868, however, that the mill was redesigned with new furnaces and the flue extended. It had a short period of prosperity and the freeholders shared the profits which soon exceeded the cost of the mill. It finally closed in 1886 and since that date the mines have ceased to be important in the assets of the Trust Lords.

The net effect of government by Trust Lords has been the creation of a real sense of independence and self-reliance, coupled with an active interest in all the affairs of the township and manor.

Conistone is the township neighbouring Kettlewell on the south, that is downstream. The southern boundary of Kettlewell crosses the Wharfe valley by the crest of a terminal moraine, climbs the nose of Knipe, the fell between Wharfedale and Littondale, and drops down to the Skirfare, the river of Littondale. The centre of the river is then the whole of Conistone western boundary. The township runs about 3 miles down the river and stretches about $4\frac{1}{2}$ miles up to the watershed. The river is about 600 ft O D at Conistone, and the fells to the watershed rise to just over 1,800 ft O D. Nearly three-quarters of the township is above 1,000 ft O D and is rough pasture leading up to heather moorland. The River Skirfare joins the Wharfe just below the Kettlewell boundary. Unlike Kettlewell, Conistone lies entirely on the east side of the river (Illus. 12, Fig 5).

At the time of the Domesday Survey there was a single manor which passed in time to the de Romille family of Skipton, and Alice de Romille granted it to a Saxon family which took the name of de Hebden, from the place Hebden, separated from Conistone by the township of Grassington. Conistone remained in the family of de Hebden for most of the monastic period, with no monastic property but a single house and pasture for 500 sheep within it. In the mid-fifteenth century Conistone and Hebden descended by the marriage of a daughter and co-heiress to the Tempest family. The manor of Conistone was eventually inherited in the mid-sixteenth century by Richard Tempest of Bolling Hall, near Bradford, along with a dozen other manors.

This Richard Tempest was a man of affairs, deeply involved in Crown matters. His many and high offices made it impossible for him to take any personal interest in most of these manors, and the lack of a direct heir induced him to get rid of the burden of their management by sale to some of his cousins and other relatives. It was by such a sale that the manor of Conistone, in 1568, was disposed of to Alexander Rishworthe, of the Heath, near Wakefield, for £500. The deed of sale states that Tempest granted the manor with all estates, houses, cottages, buildings, feedings, lands, woods, pastures, commons and common of pasture, mines, quarries, etc, and all rights, privileges, etc,

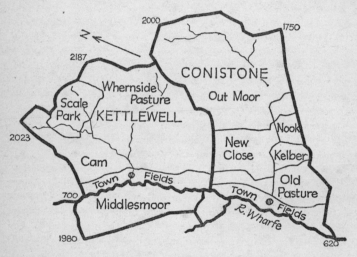

Fig 5 Kettlewell and Conistone Townships (Figures are heights above sea level)

belonging to the lordship of Conistone, and also all his deeds and charters and other evidences. Rishworthe, before April 24th next was to acknowledge a fine upon the manor, before one of the Queen's justices.

On September 21st, 1575, Rishworthe sold the manor to John Kaye of Oakenshaw, except for one tenement with its lands which he had already sold to one John Battie, its occupant. This sale was for £700 and is an example of the money which was being made at that time by sale and resale, particularly of ex-monastic estates. By this deed Kaye was to hold the manor by the fortieth part of a knight's fee paying such suit and service to the court of the manor as often as it shall be held, as other freeholders do and have been accustomed to do, and suit of mill now being within the manor or hereafter to be placed within the manor, and to pay the ancient rent to the Chief Lord.

On October 6th, 1583, John Kaye, in consideration of certain sums of money, granted to Henry Garforth, Robert Rathmell, William Topham, Henry Ibbotson, Richard Preston, Thomas Sergantson, John Nelson, Cuthbert Hill, Thomas Topham, William Procter, Thomas Smythe, Nicholas Hewitt, Thomas Hewitt, James Ibbotson, Richard Lambert, James Stapper, Henry Constantine, John Layland, William Slinger, Richard Todd, Richard Wigglesworth, William Ripley, Robert Marton, John Battie, Thomas Ibbotson, Isabel Parkinson, and George Horner all the manor and everything pertaining to it for ever. The first fourteen of these persons did not live in Conistone but acted in part as trustees, while the rest were all tenants within the manor. They were to hold the manor in trust for the sole use of their heirs and assigns and were to divide among them proportionately to their several tenements. The process of selling the tenements to the occupants was accomplished slowly, but by an indenture of October 19th, 1584, the first of them, Richard Wigglesworth, bought his tenement. In this first deed are set out in full the conditions of the sale of the various tenements, in such a manner that it was referred to in later disputes, and in 1687 as 'an Indenture of Combination amongst the Inhabitants and all the other Freeholders belonging to the said Manor of Conistone'.

Briefly it states that:

Whereas the freeholders bought the commons, moors, etc. to be divided among them proportionately to the ancient rents of £14.6.8 and all moors and commons into 288 parts divided which is after the rate of 1 part to every 12d of

ancient rent ... and whereas Richard Wigglesworth purchased all their right and estate of and in 8 parts and shall
not occupy more nor less than has been occupied in Conistone Old Pasture with the same tenement ... and all shall
agree that election be made between the 1st of March and
15th of April for the appointment of byelawmen of one of
the said parties for one year and the said byelawman may
chose yearly on the day of his election 4 inhabitants dwelling
or being owner or farmer of some part of the premises to
assist him for that year to rateing them to a reasonable Stint
of Pasture and Turbary and for all common wrongs touching
the said moors and wastes and all duties of Neighbourhood
among the owners of farms and occupiers of any of them the
said orders and byelaws being published by the said byelawman and the said four assistants ... and if any do not per-
form the said orders then they or any of them shall pay to
the Byelawman fines to be bestowed for the good of all the
owners and occupiers, such penalties within ten days ...
and if they refuse they shall be ordered by the lord president
of the Council in the North parts and shall abide such order
as shall there be set down touching the same.

This deed set the pattern of the village rule for more than
three centuries, the bylawmen, regularly appointed, setting the
stint of the pastures, regulating the commons and moors,
letting the shooting and appointing a barmaster to regulate the
mines. The constable and overseers of the poor also came under
their scrutiny, and they appointed a pinder to impound stray
animals in the pound which they built and maintained. They
were the government of the village. The old common pasture
of the village economy was overstocked and so others were
added to it. The Nook and Kelber were in fact extensions of
the Old Pasture, carrying the area farther up the fell, but were
only enclosed about 1600. Immediately the first bylawmen
began their consideration of the common pasture stints they
decided to enclose a large area of good grass on the limestone
terraces to the north-east of the common fields, separated from
them by a high limestone cliff. These areas so enclosed formed

the New Close, which in 1587 is described as 'newly enclosed'. The enclosing wall of the New Close was built by all the inhabitants and freeholders and afterwards maintained by them.

The stint decided by the bylawman and his assistants, with the help of all the village, was the total number of sheep, cattle or horses which it was thought could be grazed on the common pastures without fear of overgrazing and causing deterioration. The Old Pasture was, of course, part of the very old village economy; its stint was already traditional and the proportion of beast gates – feeding and grazing for a 'made beast' (full grown) – was already a part of each tenement and its lands and common rights. For over two centuries these common pastures each remained as single undivided enclosures and from time to time, at his discretion or on the complaint of a commoner, the bylawman and his assistants would 'drive' the pastures, that is they would gather up all the animals in each and count them. The result was entered in the township record as 'New Close driven and Accounted June 27th 1720', followed by a list of all the gateholders and the number of their beasts, such as sheep, lambs, cattle, and horses. The same was done in succeeding days for Kelber, Nook and Old Pasture.

From such lists it can be seen that, with little exception, the Old Pasture was kept for cows, Kelber for horses, New Close almost entirely for sheep, while Nook was very variable but useful as an overflow from Old Pasture, beasts with some sheep and an occasional horse. The numbers of stock vary with the prosperity of the farming and the state of the grazing in the pastures, but the common range in the eighteenth century was about 130 to 200 beasts in Old Pasture, 1,200 to 1,700 sheep in New Close, 30 to 40 horses in Kelber, and 130 to 150 sheep and some beasts or horses in Nook. An elaborate code for the regulation of the pastures was agreed in 1687 and was renewed and revised from time to time thereafter.

The first bylaw of this code called every freeholder and inhabitant to meet the bylawman and his assistants at 8 AM on a particular day, or to send a substitute, to make all fences and ditches through all the moors and pastures, and to continue at this work until all are done, on pain of 8*d* (3½p) fine in any default of such attendance. The rest of the bylaws refer to the dates on which animals could be put into the various pastures, and the number to be allowed for every 1*s* (5p) or 2*s* (10p) of ancient rent paid for the tenement. There were fines for over-stinting the pastures, and such matters were mentioned as that one beast was to be the equivalent of two stirkes (bullocks) not more than one year old, or of four sheep or half a horse. A mare and her foal could 'go on 2/6 rent'. The number of lambs to a gate changed with the season, an adjustment being made usually about June 11th when the lambs were becoming well grown.

By the sale and descent of beast gates, the proportions and their regulation had become increasingly complex, so on November 2nd, 1797, a towns' meeting decided that

> a Meeting of the owners of Cattlegates upon the said several Pastures be held at the house of Henry Ovington in Kilnsey (an inn) on Friday the Eighth day of December next at One of Clock in the afternoon, to take into Consideration the Propriety of applying to Parliament the next Session for an Act to Divide and Inclose the said Pastures . . .

In fact an Act, jointly with Kettlewell, was obtained and an enclosure award was made in 1801. The survey for this ascertained that the grazing was as follows – Old Pasture 111 beast gates, Nook and Kelber 73 and 74 beast gates, New Close 1,449 sheep gates, and Conistone Out Moor and Bycliffe New Pasture 830 and 271 sheep gates. The five pastures were divided out and allotted and much of the work of the bylawman was over.

During the seventeenth century the mineral veins which cross the edge of Conistone Moor and Mossdale began to be worked, and the bylawman became also the barmaster, to control the mines as he controlled cattle. A code of mineral laws, based on those of Derbyshire, was drawn up and all persons wishing to mine had to obtain licence from the barmaster and have his 'mere' of ground (32 yds along the vein) measured. Ore was to be dressed at the mine and to pay a royalty of $4\frac{1}{2}d$ (2p) each dish of 'wine measure three gallons and a half', or else one-thirteenth of the smelted lead. For over a century these royalties brought a small income to the freeholders, as each year the barmaster made his report and the income was shared out. A severe test of the barmaster and the freeholders came in 1721 when miners, strangers to the place, appeared on the mines and began to sink a shaft without the formality of a licence from the barmaster. To all questioning they simply said that they were mining for calamine (zinc carbonate) by authority of those who had the right to mine this ore throughout England and Wales. The Conistone men responded by filling in the shaft and telling the strangers that if they appeared again they would be buried in the bottom of any excavation they made.

The story goes back to 1564–5 when the Society of Mines Royal, which went through a long and complex history, left some of its powers finally in the hands of Moses Stringer and William Wood. They claimed that Conistone was Crown land because Fountains Abbey had owned pasture there. The freeholders countered this with a recital of their many deeds and their control of the whole manor, and after six years of the presentation of cases, rebuttals, restatements, and other legal documents running to over 300 very closely-written foolscap sheets, Wood withdrew his case and Conistone continued to control its own mines.[5]

The bylawman continued to be full of business, calling the inhabitants to attend for 'hanging ye township gates', repairing walls and roads, paying 'cesses' (local taxes), and dealing with many other matters of town government. Until the formation of the parish council of the joint township of Conistone with Kilnsey, they were the representatives of an almost autonomous local government by inhabitants and freeholders acting as lords of the manor.

CHAPTER FOUR

A yeoman farmer's house and farm

AN APPRAISAL of the features which give character to the Yorkshire dales villages would include the number of seventeenth-century buildings still in use as inhabited houses. They can be recognized by their mullioned windows, carved and often dated doorheads, stone roofs and the minor details of chimneys and gables. The field barns and other farm buildings which are contemporary have their own detail and plan which bring them into the same group and style of vernacular architecture. Examples have been photographed and many appear in the work of artists – they have been mentioned by topographers and popular writers and have acquired a descriptive term, used very widely but with too little precision, 'typical dales houses'. Actually they are a small minority, three or four remaining in a village, but they are so striking and attractive that they remain in the memory above all the other buildings of later date, although some of these are equally worthy of study and remembrance. Although the buildings are so well known, very little has ever been published about the actual individuals who built any such house – except perhaps the name indicated by the initials and date over the door – and nothing about the method and cost of building. Without being able to present a complete and finished account, we can give some details of a particular house and its history, of the building, the getting together of materials, the way its barns were built, and something of the furnishings and contents of the house. Because the house we are to study is like a hundred others in all its main features, we can perhaps accept these details as applying in general terms to many 'typical' houses.[1]

Before we turn to the seventeenth century we may ask if

domestic buildings of earlier date are to be seen and what kind
of building preceded the long mullion-windowed stone house.
Most of the stone houses belong to the seventeenth or later
centuries and almost all have replaced earlier houses which
were built of timber and thatch. However, a sufficient number
of the earlier buildings remain for us to see how they were
built and to know what they were like. These earlier buildings
are 'crucked', which means that the principal feature of their
construction is the use of pairs of curved timbers, their feet on
the ground and their tops coming together like a Gothic arch
and carrying, from pair to pair, the rooftree. There is a cross-
bracing timber at about half their height, making a frame like
the letter A. The crucks are frequently very symmetrical, as
they were often obtained by splitting a heavy curved branch or
trunk of oak or elm lengthwise, and so getting a completely
matching left and right timber.

These crucks are set up, two or more pairs of them, with low
side walls from one pair to the other, on which rest the feet of
spars or branches, their other end resting on the rooftree. This
frame will now carry a thatch roof of steep pitch. A pair of
crucks, that is two timber frames of the A shape are set up
about 10 or 12 ft from one another with a ridgetree, and are
then said to form a room of one bay width, a unit in which
early buildings were generally measured. The dimensions of a
bay remained fairly constant for a long time. Bishop Hall
described the small farmer's house as

> Of one bay's breadth, God whot a silly cote,
> Whose thatched spars are furred with sluttish soote
> A whole inch thick, shinning like black moor's brows
> Through smoke that down the headless barrel blows.
> At his bed's feete feeden his stalled teame,
> His swine beneath, his pullen o'er the beame.

The bay's breadth of 10 to 12 ft was the space required for
stalling a pair of oxen. The headless barrel formed the chimney,
placed in the thatch, lined with clay and being nothing more
than an escape hole for smoke from an open fire burning

somewhere on the earthen floor. In 1621 a Cheshire yeoman farmer was described as having his fire 'in the midst of the house against a hob of clay, and their oxen under the same roof; but within these forty years it is altogether altered so that they have built chimneys'.

In the dales area of which we are now thinking several of these early cruck buildings remain, most of them now used as barns, or – to use the local term – laithes. In a survey of Cracoe in 1586 many particulars of such buildings are given: Richard Cookson had built a 'fire house of four pair of crucks' (that would be of three bays); others had a barn of four bays, another a 'firehouse and a lath of three pair of crucks'. A little earlier, in 1569, the Court Baron of Cracoe reported many tenants 'for that they had improved one little house' or 'improved one ffyre house and a garth' and the Court proceeded to improve the rents by reassessments. In many cases the improvement had been the addition of another pair of crucks, thus making an additional bay at the end of the house.

By the sixteenth and early seventeenth centuries these ancient timber and thatch buildings were suffering decay, and as monastic tenants who purchased their farms after the Dissolution became after two or three generations more prosperous, they began to improve their properties by a more convenient and fashionable manner of building. Their replacements were in a newer style, all built in stone, though some of the smaller and detached farm buildings continued to be thatched for another century or more. There were families of builders descended from the masons who had maintained the monastic properties and who, for a few generations after the Dissolution, had found abundant occupation building bridges and some of the large houses of the monastic appropriators. These men had a traditional skill, and for a small house could work without an architect, following a simple general pattern and thus providing buildings with a close family likeness although with constant minor variations sufficient to give each house a measure of individuality. In general, the house plan followed very closely that of the crucked house of three or four bays. A large living-room, occasionally of two bays' length, the crucks now replaced by substantial load-bearing outer walls of between 2 and 3 ft thickness, with roof trusses of heavy oak spanning them, would have another bay making an end room or parlour. The larger room, usually called just 'the house' or 'house-place' was kitchen-living-room and the parlour was the bedroom of the master and mistress. The first floor, little more than a loft of rooms all opening one from the other, provided for the rest of the family and some servants. Farm men usually slept in the farm buildings. In some houses the line was continued by adding two or three bays at the kitchen end of the house, which made hay barn and cowhouse, thus making a very long low building of six or seven bays.

The fireplace was now built in an internal party wall of sufficient thickness (some have been measured as 8 ft) to carry two fireplaces back to back. The kitchen fire was accommodated within a deep arched recess of 7 or 8 ft span, miscalled an inglenook, and the parlour fire was in a smaller, often slightly more ornate fireplace. The house walls were substantial, as they had to carry not only the heavy roof trusses but the great weight of a low-pitched stone roof. All these considerations set fairly close limits of variation and secured a family pattern for the houses of a wide area.

Only the accident of preservation of a house in Conistone, with its deeds and a number of other documents, enables one to trace, by means of the documents and by analysis of the building, the history of a dwelling which retains features common to many of the dales houses. The house was built in stone in the mid-sixteenth century, of three bays' length, about 51 ft by 19 ft. It was enlarged between 1686 and 1694 by an addition of a 14 ft-wide extension behind two of the bays. A new single roof was put over the whole house, so that the massive chimney stack on the centre line of the old building is now to one side of the centre of the extended gable. The mullioned windows have been replaced by late Georgian sashes and a few partitions have altered the internal plan slightly, necessitating the making of one or two new doorways and blocking an old one. The whole front has still later been covered with cement stucco (Fig 6).

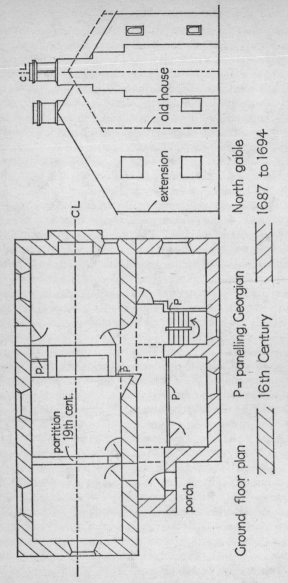

C.L

old house

extension

North gable

1687 to 1694

CL

P
P
P
P

partition 19th cent.

porch

Ground floor plan   P = panelling, Georgian

16th Century

Fig 6. A yeoman's house at Conistone built at two periods

The manor of Conistone, within the Honour of Skipton, was for some centuries held by the family of de Hebden, but by a female line it had come into the family of Tempest of Broughton (see Chapter Three for details). In 1568 Richard Tempest sold the manor with all its tenements, lands, rights, privileges, commons, pastures and wastes to Alexander Rishworth, who in turn sold it to John Kaye in 1583. Kaye almost at once began to sell all properties to their occupiers and the whole of the lordship of the manor to the freeholders jointly. It is just before this point that we can start the story, the house and tenement we are studying being one of the ancient houses of the manor.

The house stands in a close near the south end of the village, close to the hall, and has taken the name of the close, Hemplands. The cultivation of flax, its preparation and weaving into linen with the coarser hemp for harden and rope, was a widespread cottage industry throughout the dales, and Hempgarth, Hemplands and similar names are found in most villages.

In 1563, before the sale of the manor, Sir Richard Tempest demised a tenement, farmhold and messuage, with lands and all commons of pasture and use of the waste, to Richard Wigglesworth, then the tenant, to have it for twenty-one years. In 1584, at the expiry of this lease and when the manor was being sold, Wigglesworth was able to buy it with its due proportion of the lordship and manor. Three years later, by his will, his son Thomas inherited this tenement and lands and it descended in the family until in 1681 it was inherited by Richard, son of Robert Wigglesworth.

By this time the original lands that went with the house had been increased by the purchase from time to time of closes and fields; it was now one of the larger farms of the township and its owner became one of the most prosperous farmers in Conistone. In 1677 Richard married Anne Leyland, whose family was already very closely linked with the Wigglesworths, and on inheriting in 1681 he began to improve the house, judging by the scraps of carpenter's and other accounts which remain. Anne died, and in 1687 he married as his second wife another close friend, Elizabeth Topham. The year before this second marriage he planned the extension of his house and began to get together the necessary materials.

Among surviving documents there is a very fragile, tattered and incomplete book. It is of foolscap size, with pages missing at front and back, leaving only fifty-two. The edges are so torn and worn as to cut off the last words of most lines, and on many pages the prices are missing. It was a daybook or scrapbook of Richard Wigglesworth, into which he entered memoranda obviously to be used later for fair copies. The entries run from 1682 to 1700, but many items are written into any space which had been left on a page, irrespective of where in the book this was. Subjects are completely mixed up, and no discernible order is to be seen in their arrangement. There are drafts of church-wardens' accounts, some pages of constables' accounts, memoranda of amounts of fencing to be done by various free-holders, entries of the number of sheep clipped in several years, wool bought and sold, and notes of all kinds. It is obvious that Richard put down in his book his accounts when occupying some of the many township duties which came to him in rota-tion – churchwarden, constable, pinder in charge of the pound, bylawman, overseer of the poor and so on. Scattered through these are household accounts, farm notes, building accounts, the cost of funerals, recipes for medicines for animal and human illnesses, charities, and the memoranda of every kind made by a busy man not trained as a clerk and having no real system in his booking. It is from this manuscript that we can disentangle accounts for his house and barns, lists of linen and pewter at various dates, besides gaining, in the effort to disentangle them, a clear picture of the life of a very active man.

The earliest account directly connected with the house extensions starts in June 1686 with some details of the many timbers needed. The accounts are in no regular order and are, in part, written into spaces in earlier pages, but by the names and occasional dates they can be sorted into a proper order. First, timber was to be collected, because in upper Wharfedale large timber was becoming scarce. The mines had made great demands on straight timber for props and other purposes, and timber had been taken regularly for house repairs and construction. The woodland still surviving was mainly the lighter scrubby woods of the limestone scars and screes, none of it large enough for house building. The extensive woodlands around Bolton Abbey, twelve miles away, and the remaining parts of Barden Forest were the nearest source still providing large timber, and Wigglesworth would have to go there to select and buy suitable trees.

Wood & stones & glass for ye fyre house.			
paid to Sampson Lupton for two trees	4	15	0
paid more to Sampson Lupton towards three trees	0	5	0
for felling fower trees & in ale 2 one day & 3 one day	0	6	0
for quartering one great tree	0	5	0
paid for quartering & cutting one tree	0	4	0
to Christopher Broadbelt for cutting a great tree	0	1	0
in ale when we led the wood from Greear Hill	0	1	8
paid to Jo Ellis & Wm West for sawing	0	10	0

The sawing up of this timber was probably done at Barden and the carriage from there to Conistone would be a matter for Wigglesworth's own carters. On June 5th, 1686, he bought from John Piccard of Keighley a great stock of prepared timber –

eighty sparres or upwards soe many as shall suffice for a house of 19 yards in length and 21 yards of roofetrees 4 inches square and spares 4 inches deep & 3 inches in thickness for 1s 1½d a piece & roofe trees to be delivered at ye same price according to there length & all of them to be sufficient to the sight of a workman & to be delivered between (now) & ye michaelmas come twelve months at Bardenscale and ye Broadparke & 6d in earnest paid.

It would appear from this account, and from the fact that the timber was to be prepared and delivered at Barden Scale, that

Piccard was to cut up and shape it. Piccard worked in other places, evidently wherever trees had been bought.

Two Balkes bought of ye aforesaid John Piccard ye day & yeare abovesd which is to be delivered a foot square throughout & 18 foot in length in Middleton Wood in a place where it is sufficient for a Draught to come to it for fifteen shillings a piece & is to be paid at Michaelmas next when ye Balkes is delivered.

Bargained at Skipton in Anthony Naylours & to be good and sufficient to ye sight of Will: West of Conistone in ye presence of Anthony Naylour 6d being paid in earnest.

Fower pair of Sinetrees bought of ye aforesd John Piccard ye day & yeare abovesd 10 inches deep & 5 inches in thickness is to be delivered between (now) & michaelmas next for 6s 8d a paire & to be good and sufficient to ye sight of Will: West & sixpence in earnest paid.

May the 22nd in ye yeare abovesd ye abovesd John Piccard hath sould unto me one Rood of good and sufficient Quartercleft boards without either shake or sappe or any other thing which may be thought to be hurtfull to ye same to ye sight of a workman & is to delivered at Bardenscale between (now) & ye next Michaelmas for £2 10 0 paid in earnest 6d

Paid John Piccard for 80 sparres & 5 eastres pieces & 2 balkes June ye 18th ye sum of £6 0 0.

Paid for latnailes & spikings May ye 18   8s od.

paid for one hundred of latts ye same time   4s od.

paid for 3 hundred of latts ye 11th of November   13s 6d.

paid to George Lawcock June ye 24th ye sum of £4 in pte for 14 sparres & 1000 lattes 45s, & ribbes & one mould board.

As a freeholder of the manor, Wigglesworth would have the right to fetch building stone from the outmoor for repair and extension to his house, at the cost only of carting and the nominal lord's rent. The township quarries were on Bycliffe in Mossdale, with a sledge road down to Conistone, about two miles away. While getting his building stone free, the stone slates for roofing and the flags for the floors had to be bought, as quarries for these were not available at that time in the township and were leased and worked by quarrymen and slate cutters. Quarries of the better-quality slate which would be used on a house roof were at Walden Head and Starbotton Moor beyond Kettlewell, and, as with the timber, Wigglesworth ordered the slates that he would require well in advance and made arrangements for delivery dates and payment. He started in October 1685 with a memorandum

> that Thomas Harrison hath sould Twenty gaiges of sleat unto me & is to deliver it good & sufficient to ye sight of any workman between ye first day of May next ensuing ye date hereof for Two pounds & ten shillings but ye said Richard Wigglesworth is to pay ye Chiefe Lord his dues.

The gaige is a quarryman's measure of loads of slate and is variable. The slate was to be led down from 'ye hard raike in Waldenhead' to Starbotton and to be set down on the Conistone side of the mill bridge, which could only be the bridge on the Conistone side of Kettlewell. John Simonson would find a place for it to lie. They were to have 2s 6d (12½p) a gaige for leading. Another ten gaiges was got of John Harrison and John Calvert, for which, delivered as the other was, 6s (30p) a gaige and a half-peck of malt were to be paid. These were not the whole of the slates needed, as others were bought in smaller parcels, but these later amounts may have been for use on one or other of the barns and farm buildings.

The roof was now fully provided for, baulks for purlins and trusses, spars and laths with nails for slating, and the proper quantity of slates ordered. The next accounts must be for building, and in one part of the daybook there are memoranda of payments for labour:

paid to Robert Johnson & Thomas Johnson for working	0	2	10
Paid to James Stackhouse & Thomas Harrison for walling ye house	6	5	0
paid to Thomas Green for dressing ye slates		7	0

There are other similar payments for labour about the walls and roof. The ground floor was provided for by two purchases of flags from Joseph Motley, totalling 19s (95p). Daniell Tailforth was paid £2 for '6 windows & 4 lowpholes & one dubble piped chymney', and Stephen Browne supplied five casements for 12s 6d (62½p). There was still wood to be bought and prepared for the internal fitting, and a Mr Haworth was paid for '10 fir deels & one norway oak' and Mr Symnel Tenant for three 'fir deels'. John Ellis and Thomas Sergeantson were paid 6s (30p) for sawing the wood. The laths used for hanging the slates had been 'riven', not cut, by Robert Wiggon for 5s 5d (27p).

The chamber floors, doors and 'seeling' (ceiling) cost £4 and glass was got from Richard Clapham for 6s (30p). Snecks, locks and hinges were bought for 6s (30p) from Howarth, and the blacksmith made a range, a toasting-fork and curtain rods. Christopher Alcock made a round table which cost 18s (90p) and so must have been of specially good quality. It is not easy to tell how many people were paid as labourers and builders, but eight men are named as being paid for so many days of day work at 6d (2½p) a day. If this was the rate for all, then the sum of £5 18s (£5.90) paid to these men for labour not otherwise specified represented 236 days of work, an average of 28½ working days or about five weeks each. The total of all the miscellaneous accounts, including the labour, is £74 8s 9d (£74.44), so that it might not be unreasonable, in view of the way the accounts are scattered about the daybook and the almost casual nature of some of the memoranda, to suggest that the house cost somewhere about £100.

The building was completed by 1687, but in 1694 a small stone porch was added to shelter the door of the new part which faced north-east and must have been a source of many cold draughts. The door of the porch has a carved lintel with R W 1694 in a slightly sunk panel, there is a well-cut string-course round the porch, and all the mason work is of very good quality.

There is no full list of the contents of the house at this time, but in various wills of the family a few articles are mentioned,

the best bed, awmbries (cupboards), arkes (large chests), brass
pots, chairs and so on, and in 1686 there are two lists made by
Richard Wigglesworth. One is of 'Bedding left in ye Arke,
Coverlets & Pillows, wishons (cushions)'; this might be a
reliable indication of the extent of household linen, much of
which would have been spun and woven from their own flax
and possibly by the women of the family of more than one
generation. Each 'spinster' daughter was encouraged and expected to spin for her 'bottom drawer' a good supply of linen,
and many of the items in the following list may have been
brought to the house by the wives of the Wigglesworth men.

in Linning Table Cloathes one of hoggaback (huckaback) &
    one of Linning
in Sheets fower paire & one sheet hempen
in Sheets fower paire one being somewhat worn
in Pillow beares fower
in Towells three of them being with white cut work
one ballance for a bed hanging with a fringe
in haggaback napkyns two
in Linning napkyns six three being of line and three of
    Linetow
in Linning sheets three paires
in Table Cloathes two one of huggaback and one of Line
in Haggaback napkyns six
in plaine napkyns six three of line and three of linetow
in pillow beares fower
in Towells two
in hempen sheets three.

There is also, with this, 'An account of what Peuder (Pewter)
was'.

Great new dishes	12	tow candlesticks	2
of an oulder sort	11	one tumbler one salt	2
Little plaits new ones	8	one little podinger	1
& two ould ones	2	one mustard box	1
Three pewder Tankars	3	three pottingers & one	
tow salts & one oyle	2	little one	4

one flagon	1	in pewder seaven dublers	7
one pewder tumbR.	1	one flagon one candlestick	
one cup of pewder	1	one aqua vitae bottell	3

When his house was completed Richard Wigglesworth turned his attention to the condition of some of his farm buildings. During the seventeenth century much of a long area of pasture land lying between the 'great wall' or 'head wall' (both names occur in deeds and conveyances), which marked the upper limit of the arable town field north of the village and the limestone scar beyond which was the New Close common pasture, had been enclosed in 'closes' or small fields. Many of these had a laithe built in them with standings for two or three cows and room for the winter supply of hay. Occasionally a farm hind would live in a part of such a laithe, in a room made for the purpose. Wigglesworth had barns at Hillcastles and Howlebeck Closes, both in poor condition, so he decided to rebuild them. As both are typical of the scores of laithes built about that period, we might look at how they were built. One end accommodates the hay crop, and the centre bay of a three-bay laithe is kept fairly clear for storage and perhaps for a cart. The end bay has booses, standings for a few cows. The big laithe doors are in the middle bay and there may be a porch to give them a little shelter. The cow part sometimes comes forward to form one side of the porch or to make a small calf house.

There are two accounts, not easily separated, for work done about 1689. The first note is:

Howlebeck Leath lett to build with Tho: Kidd for £3 & is to make it eleaven yards in length within & five yards in breadth & seaven yards in breadth in ye shippon and fower yards high above ye earth to ye square & to breake all ye greet stone and to hew one doore.

Another memorandum says that:

Thos kidd hath taken ye laith to wall at ye rate of sixpence ye yard & is to break all ye hewen stones in at ye bargain for one rough arch & ye corner stones and hath received six-pence in earnest being December ye 27 1688.

A separate note is made when Kidd was paid 'for pulling down Howlebeck house' and £1 was advanced to him in June 1689 towards 'ye walling of ye same'. There are the usual purchases of slates and cost of leading, but nothing for timber, suggesting that the old timbers were re-used, a very common practice.

The second accounts are for Hillcastle House, a small building which has now entirely disappeared, or by being altered to a barn is now not recognizable with certainty. Again, payments were made 'for ridding groundework and pulling downe ye olde house at Hillkastle for six dayes meat and wages fower shilling'. As the normal day wage was 6*d* (2½p), this leaves 1*s* (5p) for six days' food. George Stayenforth was paid 14*s* (70p) for two gaiges of slate and for cutting stones, and Thomas Kidd got £2 12*s* 6*d* (£2.63) for walling and cutting the stones. Payment was made both for getting and leading cornerstones, slates and flags. Other items include:

James Stackhouse for sleating ye laith porch and Hillcastle house, 3*s*. getting ling leadinge & Thatching at Hillcastle house thirty shilling. William West for all ye wright worke ... £2.0.0 for ye balkes & bowses in ye olde leath.

In both cases the stone of the old building was re-used, so only the better-quality cornerstones (quoins) and arch stones had to be quarried. The Hillcastle building may have been thatched to save the cost of the much heavier timbers that would be necessary for a stone roof.

After all this involvement with the building accounts, have we any picture of the man who was responsible for them? To use all the notes and memoranda available about his many activities would require another chapter, but a brief sketch can show something of his share in the life of his village. His farm was one of the larger ones, perhaps 40–50 acres of arable, much of which he let out in small portions of 2 or 3 acres to other

farmers in the village. He did grow oats and barley and paid
for them to be dried at the town kiln, and he also paid for his
barley to be made into malt, some of which he used in brewing
his own ale and the surplus he sold. His chief interest was in
sheep, and for these he had, besides his 'enclosed' closes, many
sheep and some cattle gates on the common pastures, with, of
course, the right to use the outmoor and unenclosed common.
His memoranda include notes of 'sheep greased at mid-Aprill
1694. Hogs 26, shearlings 50, ewes 51, weathers two and three
shears 54, rams 2, hoggs bought 20', and in that year 176 sheep
were clipped. These figures are a good average over many years,
his flock varying year by year, but never much above or below
200.

Born in 1650, he was thirty-two when his daybook starts and
around forty when the varied activities we have discussed were
at their peak. He was a responsible owner-farmer and occupied
all the various offices of the township, some for many years and
others as annual appointments on more than one occasion. He
was churchwarden to 'Parson Alcock' for many years and more
than once was overseer of the poor. In this his most frequent
duty was that of 'passing' poor people, soldiers and cripples,
who were being returned to the parish of their birth. This duty
included providing or finding overnight accommodation,
meals, and transport for the lame.

ffor 2 travaillers with a passe relieved with meate drinke & lodg. & carr. to Kettlewell		8
ffor a woman & 3 children with a passe relieving with meat drinke & lodg. & carr. to Gress: (ington)	1	0
ffor relieving a cripple & carr. to Gressington		7
for carr. 7 in a cart to Kettlewell	1	0

In one year eighty-one travellers were fed and carried and
most of them found an overnight lodging.

In the years when he served as constable his duties were
varied, but the area was peaceful, so his journal has no record
of violence or theft. It has plenty of records of stray animals
taken into the pound or 'pinfold' at the centre of the village,

where there is also a little building to serve as cowshed and stable for stray cattle and horses. There are some closes and a road up to the common called Pinder Stile, where a large number of sheep could be accommodated; the use of this was the reward for the pinder's services. He records in great detail his captures, and accounts for the fines levied for their redemption. One example will suffice.

> One black weather with a stroake over ye backe & downe ye flanke also a stroake downe ye nearer side of ye ribbs & C & an H on ye near horn shee came to mee about ye first day of December 1684.

The year 1690 saw a different duty, when he was charged as constable to make 'An Account of ye Armes for ye Millitia'.

> paid in exchange of A Muskett 2s 6d & for a claspe for ye sword scaberd 2s 6d
> for goinge to Skipton about ye Armes for a new order 4s od
> for 4 days pay 6s for Muster pay 6d for powther & ball 1s.

In 1687 we come across him as assistant bylawman, sharing in

> Bylaws agreed & condescended upon . . . in & throughout all ye Moores & pastures belonginge any part of ye whole Manner of Conistone . . . beinge set downe & expressed.

There were thirteen regulations for the usage and management of all the commons and common pastures.

In addition to the public duties which he undertook, Wigglesworth was frequently asked to be a trustee or executor of a will, or with someone else to make the inventory and valuation of a deceased person's goods and chattels. As executor he kept accounts which throw much light on the funeral customs of the time. For the funeral in 1686 of a Conistone farmer he paid:

To Will. Stackhouse for 2 weathers & 2 lambes	1	13	0
to Issabell Clarke of gressington for white bread	0	3	0
to Ffrancis Coulton of Threshfield for spices	0	5	0
to Christopher Ibbotson of Kettlewell for rie bd.	0	1	0
to Will. West for ye Coffin & one day working	0	8	6
to Robert Ibbotson for his service	0	2	0
to Rich Battie for ye grave making	0	0	6
to Mr John Wade for a Certificate	0	0	6
to Mr Lancaster for ye ffuneral sermond	0	8	0
ffor proving his will	0	17	6
divided among ye poore	2	10	0

In all items except meat this follows the general pattern –
usually less meat was bought and its place taken by cheese and
butter. There is never any provision for drink, but the spices
would be to spice the home-brewed ale. There are several
accounts both for relatives' funerals and for those of farmer
friends. He seems to have been a popular executor.

Richard died in 1713 and left his house and properties to his
brothers Thomas and William, his wife Elizabeth having died
in 1710. Thomas, who had remained at the farm while his
brother William became a very prosperous tanner at Cottingley
in Airedale, died in 1741 and everything went to William.
When William died in 1768 he had a large estate, partly in
Bolton Abbey and Otley and partly in Conistone. He was
unmarried, so left the Conistone houses and lands to two of
his close friends: Hemplands, and the land which went with it,
to Richard Horner and his son George, who had lived in the
house as tenants under Thomas and William; and his other
house and lands in Conistone to Robert Topham of his
mother's family. George Horner followed very much the pattern of Richard Wigglesworth, deeply involved in every aspect
of service to the township and very active as barmaster of the
mines. The Hemplands property descended from him to the
present owner, and is occupied by a tenant farmer who cares
for it with a pride worthy of the many generations who have
carried it through the centuries.

CHAPTER FIVE

Country lime kilns

A CHARACTERISTIC attitude of most eighteenth- and nineteenth-century visitors to the dales was the search for the
'romantic' in scenery or for what Thomas Hurtley, the
scholarly but humble master of Malham village school, was
inspired to write about as 'Natural Curiosities'.[1] He says:

> I can only hope that this little book may be considered as
> some guide or amusement to the lovers of Natural Curiosities
> in their researches amongst as superb and stupendous
> objects as Creation perhaps can boast of ... It is no
> longer either vulgar or derogatory to the character and
> pursuits of the polite world to visit, to admire, to decorate,
> or pourtray the native elegance or majestic scenery of
> our Clime ... Craven is a very extensive and romantic
> district.

The writers of nineteenth-century guidebooks often used
the language of romance and saw the dales as a succession of
'picturesque' scenes, each self-contained as though within its
own frame in a picture gallery.

Only one traveller, Bray,[2] noted the abundant and persistent
presence of the stone walls which now are an integral part of
every scene, and the equally ever-present lime kilns. The walls
were being built and the lime kilns were in activity, but Bray
had a far more matter-of-fact attitude to the countryside than
his contemporaries and was not a romantic. The walls and
kilns are two elements so common in the view that the eye and
mind of the visitor are very apt to overlook them, to take them
for granted, and to experience little curiosity as to their origin

and purpose or their place in the social and economic history of the area.

None the less a few visitors are stirred to ask who built the walls and, looking with more care to the detail of the scene, have noticed, as they follow the run of the walls to the higher ground, the squat tower-like structure of an old kiln. Looking like the stump of some building, with the dark arch, often 'Gothic', at its base, a well-built kiln invites examination; once recognized, the persistence over wide areas becomes apparent and the signs of neglect or ruin mark the kiln as something from an earlier generation. What is it? How did it work? Who built it and why? These questions are still being asked by the more curious visitor, and the failure to find a satisfactory answer has shown that only a careful study and survey could save from oblivion the story of these humble 'monuments' of a past usage (Illus. 13).

The kilns of this study belong mainly to the eighteenth and nineteenth centuries and have mostly been disused for more than a century. Although from area to area there are variations in their superficial detail, so that kilns in one dale may appear to have a local 'fashion' distinct from those of the next, some round, some square, with arches rounded, flat or pointed, they have a basic structure dictated by their purpose and method of operation. This is capable of little variation. Their basic function is to burn limestone to lime, and this is done either in one single burning of a large quantity or in a continuing process in which limestone is fed to the kiln and lime drawn from its base, regularly and repeatedly over a longer or shorter period. These two methods are accomplished in a *pye kiln* or *pit*, or in a *running kiln*. It is the running kiln which uses the structure popularly known as the lime kiln or field kiln.

The commonest form of the field kiln is a sturdy structure of dry limestone walling forming a circular or square tower, about 15 ft or more in diameter and about the same or a greater height. There is, of course, a great variety of a few feet either way in these very average dimensions. The core of the structure is a circular bowl 8 ft to 10 ft in diameter, lined with sandstone, parallel-sided for the first 6 ft or 8 ft of its depth, and then for another 8 ft or so tapering to a bottom diameter of not more than 3 ft. At the bottom of the bowl a grate was inserted through which burnt lime and ashes could be raked out. The grate was at the end or top of a short tunnel, the mouth of which is the arch which gives the kiln its unmistakable character. The kiln is usually near the small scar or quarry from which its limestone supply could be wheeled with the greatest economy of labour.

The product of the kiln, of whichever kind, is used in two principal ways – either to make mortar for building or to spread on the land as a manure and to reduce the acidity of a sour soil. The builders' kiln rarely remains, as it was commonly set up at or near the site of a large building – church, bridge or castle – and removed after the completion of the contract. In recent times the builders' lime has come from big-scale multiple-purpose commercial kilns. The lime for the farmer was produced in the multitude of small field kilns, usually set up and operated by the farmer himself, though where conditions were suitable at the height of the demand for lime, 'selling kilns' were established where two or three men were continuously employed as 'lime burners' and where farmers without a kiln of their own could buy what lime they wanted.

Although the optimum period of the kiln was probably 1750 to 1850, it has a long 'pre-history' coupled with the increasing appreciation of the value of lime in husbandry. If we glance briefly at its earlier use we find that the preparation of lime by burning limestone or chalk in a kiln of some sort can be documented from the thirteenth century, particularly from the building accounts of many castles and some bridges. At Ogmore, Glamorgan, an early kiln has been fully excavated and dated to the late thirteenth century. It was a circular structure, a wall 6 ft thick, built with unmortared stone and enclosing a circular space 5 ft 8 ins in diameter at the ground and 6 ft 8 ins in diameter at the top of the walls which are now only 2 ft 9 ins high. This suggests that when the structure was complete the interior was probably a tapered bowl and the whole kiln of much greater height than now remains.[3] On opposite sides at the base there are wind-tunnels 4 ft 5 ins wide at the outside, narrowing to 1 ft 3 ins at the inside of the kiln. They are 1 ft 9 ins high and corbelled over with large flagstones. The floor of the kiln, when excavated, was still covered with fragments of coal and lime and there was a layer of coal ashes and lime out-side, to 18-in thickness.

The excavators of this kiln make comparisons with many other similar examples and conclude that it is of the normal pattern used in that period. Kilns of this small type and pattern remained in use until the end of the sixteenth century. George Owen, in 1595, described the Pembrokeshire lime kilns as follows:

> After the limestone has been broken into small pieces it is put into a kill made of wall sixe foot heighe foure or five foote braode at the bryme but growing narrower to the bottom, havinge two lope holes in the bottom which they call the kill eyes; in this kill first is made a fier of Coales or rather Culme which is but the dust of the coales which is laid on the bottom of the kill, and some few sticks of wood to kindle the fier.

The most abundant mention of lime kilns is in the State papers for the thirteenth and fourteenth centuries, when re-pairs and alterations were being made at the Tower of London and at many towns and castles under the king's jurisdiction. It is common to find entries in the liberate rolls and fabric rolls in the form of an order to a sheriff or constable to have a kiln made for a particular building job.

> 1228 April 24. To the Sheriff of Oxford. Contrabreve to cause a limekiln for the works of Oxford Castle to be made where most convenient, out of the brushwood that the King has ordered H. de Neville to cause the sheriff to have in a suitable place near Oxford for this purpose.

The confirmation of this order in 1229 apportions twenty-six acres of timber for the use of two kilns, one for work at the castle and the other for work on the city walls. Another example relates to Yorkshire.

> 1288 May. The Sheriff of York to cause two kilns for making lime to be made in order to enclose the bailey of Pickering Castle.

The sizes and costs of the early kilns vary, but they were by no means all small. Robert de Catteshall, Sheriff of Lincoln in 1229, spent twenty marks on making a lime kiln for the works on Lincoln Castle. At the Tower of London John, son of Andrew, was given £20 to make a lime kiln for a thousand loads of lime, and another kiln was to be made without delay to 'contain at least 2,000 loads of lime'. It is likely that these accounts refer to pye or pit kilns and are the cost of getting and piling limestone and timber and of burning and dismantling the kiln. Some accounts, however, relate to more permanent structures, as at York, where 3,300 bricks and 33 loads of clay were to be supplied for making a kiln.

In monastic building accounts kilns and lime are frequently itemized, though they are disappointing when one seeks details of the structure of the kilns. In the Pennines, Bolton Priory, as early as 1298, began to include in its Compotus such items as coals for burning lime ('In carb. marin. ad calcem ardend' xviis'). In accounts for the grange of Fountains Abbey at Kilnsey in Wharfedale, about 1446, lime was a product sent to other granges for making plaster and for building repairs. Smith[4] suggests that

> the second element (in the name Kilnsey) may, however, be O.E. *saege* 'a swamp, marsh,' referring to the wide stretch of low-lying land alongside the River Wharfe where the valley opens out; in that case the first element may well be *cyln*, possibly denoting a lime-burning kiln. 'Marsh near the kiln.'

As the name occurs in the Domesday Survey, this kiln site may be pre-Norman. The lime kilns so far mentioned have all been connected with building, and most of them were constructed for the demands of a particular job and might rarely be used again, even if they were more or less permanent structures.

The greatest change in the use of lime kilns came about in the sixteenth century, when the value of lime as a manure, particularly in the improvement of sour or poor land, was discovered. Fitzherbert in his treatise on surveying, 1546, places marl, lime and dung together as the best manures for the general improvement of poor land. Owen, in 1603, says that in Pembroke the farmers have burned lime in primitive kilns during the last thirty or forty years and have found that it was most efficient when placed upon the land hot in small heaps and left to slake in the weather.

By 1639 Gabriel Plattes and, about the same time Gervaise Markham, can both say that the process of lime burning is now so well known and widely practised that it needs no detailed description. Besides being used for land improvement, it is now mentioned as a good manure or preparation for arable land before a long series of corn crops. In 1621 Henry Holmes, a farmer of Hebden in Wharfedale, left by will among his farming assets, 'one lime kilne and turves, worth 12s'.

How was the lime burned from the raw limestone? A very sound description is that given by Mortimer in 1707.[5] With slight modification and a little more precision, this description will serve for any of the eighteenth-century field kilns still to be seen.

Lime is commonly made of Chalk or any sort of Stone that is not sandy or very cold, as Freestone etc. All sorts of soft stone, especially a grey dirty coloured stone that if you break it will yield a white powder, and all sorts of Marbles, Alabaster, Slate, Oyster and all sorts of Sea Shell ... the harder the Chalk or the Stones the better is the Lime; only they require more fire to burn them; Both sorts may be burned with Wood, Coals, Turf or Fern which makes a very hot fire.

The kilns used for Chalk or Stone they commonly make in a great pit that is either round or square according as they have convenience, and big according to the quantity they want to burn, which they make wide at the top and narrow by degrees, as they come nearer to the Bottom; the Inside of the Pit they line round about the wall built of Limestone; at the Out-side near the Bottom they have a hole or door by which they take out the Ashes, and above that some have an Iron grate, which cometh close to the wall round about; but others arch it over with large pieces of Stone or Chalk; and upon this they lay a Layer of Stone, or of what else they burn in the Kiln, and upon that a Layer of Wood or Coals etc. which they repeat till the Kiln is full; only they observe that the outermost layer be always of Wood or Coals, or what they burn their Lime with, and not of what they make their Lime, to which they give Fire at the hole underneath.

Chalk is commonly burnt in twenty four hours but Stone often takes up Sixty Hours; Ten Bushels of Sea-Coal or a Hundred of Faggots three Foot long will burn forty bushels of Chalk and forty Bushels of Chalk will yield thirty Bushels of unslaked Lime ... But the Stone Lime is much the best for Land and indeed for all other uses ... they allow a Bushel to a Pole-square, or a Hundred and sixty Bushels to an acre ... they reckon that if it is carried out upon the Land hot from the Kiln, that 'tis best.

Some landed estates included in their leases clauses such as this requiring the tenant to employ

sixteen horse loads of well burned and unfallen lime or else sixteen wain loads of good and sufficient dung or manure upon every ordinary Days work with a plow ... and not take above three crops of the same ground during the said term for once so liming.

A great traveller who went all through the country with a special eye for agriculture and its improvement was Arthur Young who became Secretary of the first Board of Agriculture. In 1770 he says:[6]

Lime throughout most parts of the North is what they

principally depend on, the benefit they urge to be great, and considering they use only *stone* lime, it is doubtless so ... upon black moorish soils the use is exceedingly great, much more so than on any other land.

When he was near Belford, Northumberland, he noted that

Discoveries of coal led to the burning of lime for the purposes of agriculture, as a manure, in a much larger way than had been usual; and for this work three new lime kilns were erected, in a most substantial manner, and at great expence.

The value of lime in the recovery of moorland attracted his attention and he became interested in the amount of 'intake' land which he saw in the northern dales. Intake is land on the upper edge of the cultivated land which is first enclosed and then redeemed from a rough vegetation of heather, sedges or bracken, or useless grasses. Draining and liming are the principal means of recovery, producing reasonable results at the cost of great labour (Illus. 14). The intakes were a particular feature of the mining areas where some of the larger companies, the London Lead Company in Alston Moor, and the Beaumonts in Allendale and Weardale, encouraged their miners to acquire smallholdings of hill ground, much of which were intake. The health of miners benefited by having a proportion of outdoor work, and poor wages were helped out by the milk from a cow, the rearing of a few sheep, or the overwintering of a few hill cattle. Only very exceptionally was intake land situated where it could be ploughed, though sometimes one or two croppings were used as a means of breaking up and cleaning.

The head of Wharfedale is formed by the junction of two moorland valleys, those of Outershaw Beck and Greenfield Beck. The Greenfield valley floor is about 1,300 ft OD at its head and 1,070 ft OD at the junction, and its enclosing hills are moorland, in part rising above 1,900 ft OD. The valley, both floor and sides, is heavily shrouded in thick glacial boulder clay and the vegetation is very rough grass and rushes. However, well up this valley one comes across a farmholding surrounded by meadows which pass on the fellsides into enclosed pastures of far better quality than any part of the surroundings. This holding is Greenfield, won from the moorland in the eighteenth century in a way which caused Young to make a big diversion in his tour to see it, and to quote it as an example to be followed. The farm was a 'contiguous tract of 2,080 acres of moorland, the rent of which was £60 a year'. The plan of the proprietor was to enclose and improve a field every year. To deal with black, moorish soils, he pares and burns and then limes it, then sows two years with turnips. After this the field is laid down to grass. He often limes for every crop, either grass or sometimes oats. The grass turns out very profitable pasture, keeps milch cows, horses, small fatting beasts, sheep, etc, very well.

As the advantages of liming became more widely known, and as the droving trade brought herds of Scottish cattle into the area with graziers seeking winter pasture for them, more and more farmers who had limestone on their land built for themselves small field kilns or cleared the land of boulders and accumulated them for a pye kiln. For those away from limestone areas, selling kilns were built on a large scale and the lime was sold at the kiln mouth or carried and distributed by 'limers' with their trains of pack ponies.

In the later years of the eighteenth century, kilns were being built all over the limestone uplands of the Pennines, and, as a new feature, attracted the attention of a few travellers who were more interested in the social and economic aspects of the population than in romantic scenes and the landed gentry. Of these travellers Young and Bray were the most observant, and their observations were supported and supplemented by Farey, the mining engineer commissioned to prepare a report on the agriculture and minerals of Derbyshire. These three writers provide many pictures of kilns at work and some details of their structure and mode of operation.

Among other references Bray noted in Stoney Middleton, Derbyshire:

Over the town is seen the smoak of the numerous kilns, used for burning the rocks into lime for manure by means of which the most barren of these hills are fertilized. The kilns are built at the foot of the rocks from which the stone is got to be burnt; they only work in the summer except one which is constantly burning lime for a smelting cupola here.

Three strike of lime are considered a load, and from forty to fifty loads are laid on an acre. Coals are sold here for sixpence the hundredweight.

He noted that the kilns burned from 110 to 300 horse-loads in two days, sold at $4d$ ($1\frac{1}{2}$p) or $4\frac{1}{2}d$ (2p) the load. Small carts carried four loads. The kilns were worked by miners, five of whom made a partnership and took a kiln for £5 a year, working in the mines in winter. At Malham, in the Yorkshire dales, he says the limestone burnt is delivered at the kiln mouth as lime, of which 6 pecks, each containing 16 quarts, costs $7d$ (3p). It takes a week in burning, and when it begins to be calcined the lowest stratum is drawn out at the mouth and more stone and coal put in at the top (Fig 7).

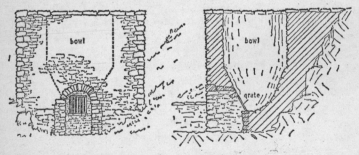

Fig 7. Field lime kiln – common square type

A more humorous aspect is provided by Hutton's description of Settle, Yorkshire.[7] He speaks of the 'white rock like a tower, called Castleber', immediately above the town and 20 or 30 yds in perpendicular height.

We were told a curious anecdote of this rocky mount. As limestone was daily got there to supply a kiln at the bottom, the inhabitants had the lime-burner presented at the court of the lord of the manor, fearing that if any more was dug out the rock might fall and bury the town in ruins, a stone having once tumbled down and broken through a garden wall beneath, in its imperious course towards the houses. Twelve wise and just men were impannelled as jurors and sent to view this impending nuisance; the verdict they returned was, that if ever it fell, it would tumble not towards the town, but the direct contrary way . . . we were informed there was a monopoly of this commodity (lime), one lime-burner or company of lime-burners having engrossed the whole of it.

Farey gives us the best description there is of the pye kiln, but his long and detailed account can be summarized. A long hollow is chosen, often against the back wall of a small quarry or scar, and here a pile of stone is raised. He describes the heap as being the shape of a boat, narrow at the base and broad at the top, if made in a 'pit', but in practice many farmers made the heap more rectangular. There is a dry-walled channel along the base with wind-tunnels leading to it. The heap, often of land clearings, is made of alternate layers of coal and broken limestone, with plenty of wood at the base. It is covered with turf, lighted, then left to burn itself out. These kilns leave little trace, except an abundance of burnt ashes and stone, and after the first land clearance a field kiln was more profitable.

Lime burning on any useful scale was dependent upon a good supply of coal which, however, need be only poor in quality, too poor in fact for almost any other use. In the Yoredale Series of rocks which make up much of the dales country, the conditions are almost ideal for the lime burner. The series, over 1,000 ft thick, is a rhythmic succession of strata in this order – limestone, shale, sandstone, and occasionally a coal seam on the sandstone. This group or 'unit' is repeated time after time, piling up the great mass from which the fells and valleys are carved out. On top of all this, on the higher fells, lies the Millstone Grit Series, coarse sandstones and shales, though in the dales area only the lower strata of the series form a capping to many of the fells. In the Yoredales the lower limestones are generally thicker and purer, and as one ascends in the series, that is, climbs higher up the hills, thin coal seams sometimes occur in the shales and sandstones. Also in the base of the Millstone Grit one or two seams of coal are found, one at least of medium to good quality. For burning lime the limestone needs only about a quarter of its weight of coal, so it was providential that the coal of the high fells could be carried downhill to the kilns placed on the lower and better limestones, which throughout the dales make long terraces and scars along the valley sides. The best of the terraces are generally along the edge separating the rough and moorland pastures from the enclosed and cultivated fields. For a purely local use the kiln might be placed at the upper limit of a farm's fields, and a downhill carriage of all materials was then the rule – coal from the higher fell down to the kiln, limestone from the scar behind and above the kiln top, lime to the fields below.

The great mass of Fountains Fell at the head of Airedale and Wharfedale has a thin cap of Millstone Grit with coal seams at no great depth. Here, towards the end of the eighteenth century, the coal began to be worked, the better quality for use at mines, smelt mills and farms, and the poorer quality for lime burning. By 1810 numerous shafts had been sunk, and a more convenient road built to replace rough and indeterminate pony tracks down the fellside.

The Rt Honble Lord Ribblesdale To fountans fell Collery
From May 7th 1810 to Oct 30th 1810
To John Brotherton and David Leman &
    Co to sinking a pit on fountans fell 6 fathom
    2 feet at 40/– per fathom   12 13 4
To Edward Watson to Banking and Making
    road to the new pit 114 days at 3/– per   17 2 0

The coal was sold as fire coal, smithy coal and lime coal, the

latter for lime burning, and quantities are fairly high. In the
year 1810,

To 674½ Load of fire coal sould at /11d per	30	18	3½
To 370 Load of Smythy coal at 1/– per	18	10	0
To 105 Load of lime coal at /7d per	3	1	3
To 55 Load of Lime coal to Lime Kiln by Wm Malenson			
To 515 Load of Lime coal remains on the Brow			
Sould to Joseph Boothman 114½ Load of Lime coal for /7 per load	3	6	9½

At the colliery a total of 7,905 loads of coal were mined that
year, of which 2,274½ were sold as lime coal and 3,033½ loads
remained on the pit brow awaiting sale or delivery. In the
following year 10,513½ loads were raised, about half of it for
lime burning. A large proportion of the lime coal was sent to
selling kilns at Settle and Malham, and the rest was fetched by
neighbouring farmers for use in their small field kilns. This
colliery remained in work until about 1880, by which time it
was supplying greater demands from some of the new large-
scale quarry kilns near Settle.

There were many other collieries in the Yoredale and
Millstone Grit rocks which opened in the eighteenth and
flourished in the early nineteenth century. They found it
possible to continue only because the relatively high proportion
of very poor-quality coal found a ready sale with the lime
burners and the better-quality coal went as 'fire coal' to the
many remote farms and hamlets. Some collieries were not
much more than local pits linked with a kiln; one such was the
subject of a lease at Conistone in Wharfedale in 1804.

23 June 1804 A Memorandum of Agreement made between John Lambert of Grassington and the proprietors of
Conistone (the freeholders); this Agmt is for Conistone
Liberty for getting coals ... John Lambert is to have the
whole Liberty for the term of 8 years paying one pound one

shilling per year and to have the privilege of building a lime-
kiln and to sell lime and coal as he can to the best advantage
... The Proprietors is to be supplied with lime & coals if
required before the outners (strangers) and suppose the
coals should not turn out for the use of burning lime the
said J.L. to be loose from any rent and deliver the same up to
the Proprietors.

Of the large collieries, that on Garsdale Common, Yorkshire,
is fairly typical (Fig 8). The coal is a fairly good seam below the
Main Limestone which makes much of the surface of the
common. The numerous shafts, now only green shaft heaps,
are widely spaced and linked by small green roads to the
Galloway Gate. This is an ancient road, in parts still a green
road, which for centuries was a highway for packhorse traffic
between Lancaster and the north. In part it was a branch of a
drove road for cattle coming from Galloway in Scotland to the
large Pennine cattle fairs. While much coal was carried by
packhorses, about 1790 small carts were coming into use, and
Professor Sedgwick, the great geologist, a Dentdale man, could
remember

when the carts and carriages were of the rudest character;
moving on wheels which did not revolve about their axle;
but the wheels and their axle were joined so as to revolve
together. Four strong pegs of wood fixed in a cross beam
under the cart embraced the axle-tree, which revolved between the pegs, as the car was dragged on, with a horrible
amount of friction that produced a creaking noise, in the
expressive language of the Dales called JYKING.
The friction was partially relieved by frequent doses of
tar, administered to the pegs from a ram's horn which hung
behind the cart. Horrible were the creakings and jykings
which set all teeth on edge while the turf carts or coal-carts
were dragged from the mountains to the houses of the
dalesmen in the hamlets below.

In 1820 a traveller in Craven says, when travelling by horse

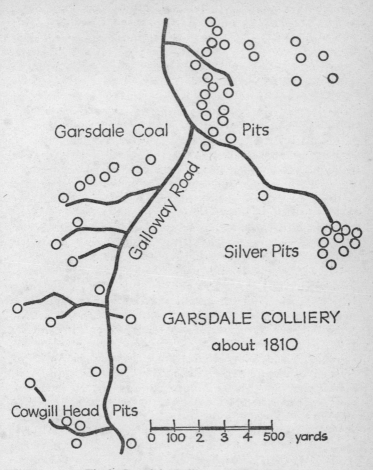

Garsdale Coal Pits

Galloway Road

Silver Pits

GARSDALE COLLIERY
about 1810

Cowgill Head Pits

0 100 2 3 4 500 yards

Fig 8. Garsdale Colliery. About 1810

from Kirkby Lonsdale to Ingleton, 'the number of small carts
laden with coal, and each dragged by one sorry horse that we
met was surprising to a stranger. Half the small farmers
between Kirkby Lonsdale and Kendal earn half their bread

with carrying coals, during most part of the year ... for fuel and burning lime in order to manure their land'. From the limestone areas around Skipton one of these ancient roads goes deep into the Millstone Grit country and is called Limers' Gate, and has along it interesting places like Slippery Ford, Limers' Croft and so on.

The remains of many collieries are a feature of parts of the higher ground, the neglected green track tempting one up the fellside only to branch in confusing pattern among a number of small pit heaps, now grassed over. It is rare that any building remains; few were used, and where there was winding from a shaft it was done with a jack-roller – two wooden uprights with a roller between them round which the rope was wound. The collieries have left a pattern on the ground, and the kilns a masonry structure which is often very attractive. Together, however, through the labour of unknown and nameless men, they have given us much of the better hill farmland and intake.

How many kilns are to be seen? An observant visitor cannot avoid seeing some, perched along the hillsides or near the track he is using, but many are so placed near a limestone scar, in the bottom of an old quarry or near the moorland edge, that few people will come near to appreciating their true number.

In a small area near the heart of the dales, the upper parts of Wharfedale and Wensleydale, above Hebden and Askrigg respectively, and in the two small dales of Dentdale and Garsdale, all four traversed by popular roads and having an abundance of tracks for the walker, 336 kilns can still be seen and these cannot by any means be thought to be all there are. A more detailed survey of all nooks and corners would find more, and would also find the flattened remains, the small quarry, the nearby hollow with plenty of burned stones, mainly from the sandstone lining of a kiln, and the half-obliterated track leading down to the fields. The number varies from township to township but can be surprisingly large. In Grassington township, Wharfedale, there are twenty-one to be found; in Dent township there are still thirty. Nearly all these are placed just below the outcrop of the thinner limestones of the Yoredale Series and many of them are not far from the thin coals at the base of the Millstone Grit.

The distribution is by no means an even spread over the area. Where easily obtainable or abundant coal occurs, the kilns tend to be numerous on the nearer suitable limestones and many of these are selling kilns. Also, the farmers within relatively easy reach of cheaper coal were encouraged to make their own kilns, however small they might be. Because of these factors, and because of the nature of the land, a distribution map of kilns would be patchy and of very variable density.

In the latter part of the nineteenth century, lime burning became a large-scale technical process demanding capital investment, and new and large industrial demands, particularly in the chemical and metallurgical industries, led to the opening of quarries on a hitherto undreamed-of scale, with banks of huge stone-built kilns, themselves soon to be replaced by steel-built monsters (Illus. 13). This new phase of the lime-burning industry was dominated by transport and congregated on the periphery of the dales, near railway and canal communication; coal was brought from the large coalfields of Yorkshire and Lancashire and collieries and kilns in the dales sank into quiescence. One by one the small kilns were abandoned and forgotten and the plume of smoke and the bright eye of the kiln were lost from our dales hillsides, never to return.

CHAPTER SIX

Water-mills and water power

ALL THROUGH the dales there remains the evidence that in former times there were a large number of water-mills, and in the documented history of the Middle Ages they are a frequent subject of grants or litigation from the twelfth century onwards. Almost every feudal manor had its cornmill to which the tenants were bound to take their corn for grinding, and in the fourteenth-century poll tax returns almost every village had its 'Miller' or 'Milner' surname, less frequently its 'Walker' or the bare professional name of 'Fuller'. The plain Miller had the water cornmill and Walker was the operative of the fulling mill, where cloth was being finished by being fulled or walked.

These early mills were small buildings of timber, not likely to survive the centuries, and either from decay or replacement they have gone. But in going many left marks which can still be recognized, or names still found as clues in most townships – Mill Lane (almost everywhere), Mill Foss (Malham), Mill Scar Lash (Kilnsey), Mill Gill (Askrigg) and many other mill combinations. On the River Wharfe and in the parish of Linton, where three of the four townships which make up the parish meet, and where the church stands in a bend of the river nearly central to them all, there are four mills or their remains which can tell a long and fairly typical story. Two streams which have run through the villages of Linton and Threshfield unite as Captain Beck and run into the river on its south side. About 400 yds above the river junction on Captain Beck a goit or leat, a cut channel, leaves the beck and, if its mouth were not now blocked off, it would carry a supply of water along its course. For some distance this goit is cut in part through rock – at about 150 yds along its course there is the shaped space in the

rock for a penstock, or sluice, so arranged that when the sluice
was closed the water was turned aside, escaped over a sill and returned to the beck. If the sluice was open the water continued to
run another 100 yds into a small dam, long since drained and now
converted into a rather attractive sunk garden. This dam is on a
bank about 30 ft above the level of the river, and below it but
built against it is the old mill, now converted into a house. In
this building there are the remains of the wheelpit, and until
the conversion the position of the millstones was obvious. One
millstone remains now as the front step of the house and fragments of another are built into the garden walls. A short goit,
partly filled in, can be traced from the bottom of the wheelpit
to the beck.

All this is a very common arrangement throughout the dales,
and a surprising number of tributary streams still have traces
of goit, dam, mill and tail race, mostly to be found with a little
careful search. This mill, still known by the older people as
Billy Gudgeon Mill from a miller, the last of a family who
worked it for more than a generation, is documented from the
thirteenth century. In the poll tax of 1379 there seems to have
been a fulling mill as well, as Thomas Milner and Thomas
Walker both paid the tax in Threshfield. In the sixteenth
century the cornmill fell into decay and in 1607 the Earl of
Cumberland leased to Rafe Radcliffe of Threshfield Hall

all that parcel of ground which was the site of a decayed
water corn mill in a close called Greenholme or Greenhawe,
of an ancient yearly rent of 33/4d, and liberty for Radcliffe to
build another mill there and also all dams, water courses,
goits, . . . and the places where the mill has been accustomed
to windo (winnow), cleanse and dress their corn and grain
brought to the said mill and suite, soke, multure, toll of the
manor . . . in as large a manner as before . . .

This seventeenth-century reconstructed goit, dam and
buildings are the features which still remain, being all built in
good stone. It remained a cornmill until late in the nineteenth
century.

Just below the entry of Captain Beck the Wharfe plunges over the Linton Falls, and on the high limestone bank and across Captain Beck from the mill just described is the site of Linton Mill. A mill here was valued in 1258 at 5s (25p) a year, and Rogerus and Henricus Milner were servants of the manor along with Willelmus Dawney, 'ffulo' (fuller), so we can picture two mills perched on this bank and probably taking their water from Captain Beck in a way similar to the Threshfield mill. At an early date, however, the power of these mills was increased by building a dam across the river near the top of the falls and making a short goit from this, thus getting the advantage of a flow of water that could hardly ever be diminished by drought. The dam is built on a long slant across the river, and so is 100 yds long although the river is only 40 yds wide. It is built of large boulders and rough walling in timber framing, some of which can still be seen in spite of subsequent and repeated repairs.

This dam is typical of many which, when built, were a source of trouble, sometimes with rioting and appeals to the Court of Star Chamber. The centre line of the river was commonly the boundary between different manors, and half the dam could be regarded as trespassing on the other manor unless very explicit agreements were made before it was built. At Litton on the Skirfare, a major tributary of the Wharfe, the Abbot of Fountains received the gift of Litton Mill in 1279. The land on the opposite side of the river was held by Salley Abbey and there was a dispute. 'For the violence and damage done by the monks and lay brothers of Salley to the Abbot of Fountain's mill in Litton' they were fined £10 'and because the dam of the mill partly extends within the common of the Abbot of Salley, he and his tenants of Litton ought to grind at the mill at the 24th vessel if they wish'. Throughout the Middle Ages these mill quarrels were common all over the country. Linton Mill was fortunate to avoid them.

Less than half a mile below Linton Mill on the north bank of the river an underground stream emerges in a very powerful spring as Brow Well. There is room between the spring and the river bank for a dam at a height from which water could be

taken for the wheel of Grassington Low Mill. In the seventeenth
century a smelt mill was built on the river bank against the
Low Mill and took a modest portion of the water for the wheel
which drove the ore hearth bellows, until 1790, from the Brow
Well stream, as it and the Low Mill belonged to the same
manor. The smelt mill is entirely ruined, but fragments of
wall, traces of the wheelpit and heaps of slag can still be seen
(Illus. 15).

The three cornmills are approached from their several
villages by contemporary ways – Grassington Mill has its Mill
Lane, part of it now absorbed in newer roads but the last
quarter-mile still a narrow deep-sunk lane, typical of any
bridle road. From Threshfield a bridle track makes a straight
line across the fields to its mill, while the Linton Mill road,
except for the last 200 yds, is now disguised in the modern
county road, though in places where there has been straighten-
ing, curves of the old track can still be seen in the fields alongside. If we may anticipate the later history of these mills, they
provide a fair picture of what happened to many similar mills
all over the dales area. Threshfield continued the longest as a
cornmill, in the nineteenth century grinding much 'proven' –
the dales word for cattle and hen food. By the opening of the
twentieth century it was a 'creamery', processing milk; then,
as this occupation ceased, it became outhouses to the mill-
house and finally was altered into a dwelling-house. Linton
Mill, when corn ceased to be ground in the eighteenth century,
became after extensions a worsted-spinning mill, then at the
mid-nineteenth century a cotton-weaving mill made redundant
and closed in the 1950s. Grassington Low Mill had a more
varied career, worsted spinning, silk and cotton, then soap-
making, wood turnery and now only a mill in name and
structure, with the dam drained and occupied by hen cabins
for a poultry fattening and dressing business.

In the eighteenth century a revolution in agriculture was
affecting the whole country and in the dales a parallel change
was in progress. The great extension of cornland in the Vale of
York and other lowland areas, and the attraction of the increasing industrial populations in parts of Lancashire and

Yorkshire, encouraged the growth of larger markets such as Skipton, Burnley and so on. In the dales the cultivation of corn, always fairly marginal because of altitude and climate, was already giving way to stock-breeding and some dairying, the corn coming into such local markets as Askrigg, Leyburn, Grassington or Pateley Bridge from the east. As more lowland was brought into corn cultivation, the smaller dales markets were displaced by larger ones such as Skipton, Leyburn and Richmond, and larger mills took over much of the corn-milling at sites in or near the new industrial centres. The small manor mills, so widely scattered over the dales, soon found it uneconomic to fetch corn from the new markets for grinding when flour could be brought with the same effort. Thus, in the latter part of the eighteenth century, one after another mill ground to a standstill and was left with only one asset, the water right it had on its stream.

From the thirteenth century some water-mills had been used for cloth fulling. The fulling mills, however, were dependent upon the growing cloth industry and were separate from the manorial cornmills except that they frequently shared the same stream with a grant, of course, from the same overlord. It was only with the textile-machinery inventions of the second half of the eighteenth century that many former cornmills became for a time important textile mills. The growing textile industry of the West Riding had concentrated more and more around Halifax and Leeds and the race of small manufacturers, the 'clothiers' had grown up by buying in wool from wide sources and then setting it out to spin, later putting out the yarn for weaving, being themselves mainly finishers and merchants. Collectors and dealers in wool known as broggers and wooldrivers had travelled the countryside to collect wool and bring it to Halifax. The so-called Halifax Act of 1555 had legalized the continuance of the broggers and drivers who took their packhorse trains through the dales, acting as middlemen to the rising industry of the towns. They bought wool mostly in small parcels at all the outlying villages and farms and carried it into the markets for sale to the clothiers. The clothiers cleaned, oiled and carded it and then sent it out again by the broggers and drivers to almost every house in the dales for spinning. The spun yarn was again collected and carried into the small towns for weaving or to be put out to cottagers in the surrounding country.

A great change was initiated with the invention by Kaye, in 1733, of his 'flying shuttle' which greatly speeded the process of weaving. The pressure which this put upon the hand spinners was only eased by the further inventions of Hargreave's spinning frame in 1764, and then, five years later, of Arkwright's spinning 'jenny'. These could spin up to eighty threads at once and so for a time could keep pace with the quicker weaving. With the coming of Arkwright's 'water frame', driven by a water-wheel, the day of the dales water-mills brightened. It seems inevitable that the broggers had a wide knowledge of the water-mills of the dales, and that either on their own or through their principal yarn merchants and clothiers they saw the possibilities of some of these mills for the new 'water frame'. Old systems of agriculture were changing, the enclosure of fields and commons had got under way, sheep and cattle were demanding less labour than corn, and these changes, along with the increasing population, created a pool of labour in the rural areas. The speculator who could secure the lease of an old water-mill with all its water rights had the ideal place in which to set up a few spinning frames.

The inventions were made in the cotton industry in Lancashire, but within a few years the turnpike roads and the Leeds and Liverpool Canal brought cotton within reach of part of the Yorkshire dales, and its distribution to the new mills presented no great problem. In this way the converted mills in the dales formed for some time an outlier of the Lancashire cotton industry, while the wool still went from the dales to feed the Halifax and Leeds industry. For many of these mills cotton manufactures formed only a brief last chapter to their long story.

Kettlewell Mill can be taken as a fair example of the involved story of such a mill.[1] A water-mill there was let to Wymerus the Miller who held it with a toft on which his house was built early in the thirteenth century. It was the property of the lord of the

manor, Robert de Grey, and in 1293 was valued at 20s 6d
(£1.025). In 1379 John Miller and Thomas Millerson were the
millers. One moiety of the mill was given to Coverham Abbey
along with a moiety of the manor, and at the Dissolution this
passed to the Crown; the other moiety became part of the
estates of the Nevilles of Middleham. The forfeiture of the
Neville properties brought both moieties into Crown possession, but the two halves were not re-combined. When the
manor was sold to the trustees for the freeholders in 1656 (see
Chapter Three), the mill dues were reserved to the trustees
but the mill itself was sold in two portions. One was bought by
the Bolland family of Kettlewell and remained in their possession
as millers for 140 years. The other was bought eventually by
Edward Prest, a mining speculator and investor, but it soon
passed by mortgage and marriage inheritance to William
Alcock, lawyer and banker of Skipton, and others. In 1792
both were for sale and they were bought by John Whitehead,
a corn factor of Marsden in Lancashire who ran the whole as
one of his several cornmills, but by 1802 he was a bankrupt and
the mill was standing unused.

The mill had two cottages, and in 1805 Richard and William
Calvert of Kettlewell leased them and converted them into a
'cotton manufactory'. The following year they bought the
whole mill, put in machinery and set up as cotton manufacturers. Until 1856 the mill continued to make cotton goods,
then was closed, never to work again. After the closure it stood
for many years, no use being found for it, and finally it was
pulled down and its stone used in other building. Its site is
now a small garden, and traces of its goit are becoming more
difficult to find as new gardens spread across it and sections are
filled in.

A mill with a comparable history is that of Malham in
Airedale. It stood in one of the most romantic situations for
which the poet or novelist could ask. Only about a third of a
mile from the magnificent Malham Cove, a limestone cliff
240 ft high and about 350 yds across the chord of its splendid
curve, the mill straddled as a bridge across the powerful
stream which emerges at the foot of the cove after a long

underground course. The stream plunges over a waterfall, at
the foot of which the mill stood, almost within reach of its
spray. The height of the fall and a slight dam across the stream
gave plenty of head for the mill-wheel, and although only
traces of the bridge foundations and of the dam and goit
remain, it is not at all difficult to re-create the impressive
picture the mill must have made when this gorge to the cove
was better wooded then it is now.

In the opening years of the thirteenth century John Aleman
gave his cornmill at Malham, with suit of 2s (10p) a year, to
Fountains Abbey for the support of the poor folk who gathered
at the abbey gate. In 1450 the bursar of the abbey valued it at
£1, and at the Dissolution it was still one of the many mills
owned and valued by the abbey. At the Dissolution it was
bought with other Malham estates but continued to work as a
cornmill. In 1680, when Thomas Atkinson had been the miller
for eighteen years, a dispute over the dues to be paid by tenants
of Malham showed that, instead of a uniform rate for grinding
corn, some tenements in the village paid one-twentieth and
some one-twenty-fourth, and these differences went back into
past history.

Early in the eighteenth century it ceased to work as a cornmill, and in 1797 it had been converted to a cotton mill and was
leased by its then owner, Brayshaw, to the three Cockshutt
brothers. In 1815 it was re-leased for twenty-four years to the
Cockshutts, along with John and Joseph Lister of Haworth,
'cotton twist spinners', but a third part was subject to a
mortgage taken by one of the brothers. The rent was £120 a
year and the mill structure, the water-wheel and pit-wheel,
upright shafts and naked tumbling shafts, with the miller's
house, dam, goit and other appurtenances, were to be insured
against fire for £2,400. The machinery in the mill was valued
at £564 and there were ancient water rents of 5s (25p) and
2s 6d (12½p) per year and a lords rent of 13s 3¾d (66½p). In this
lease we glimpse something of the arrangement of the mill
drive. The pit-wheel would be a large-diameter gear-wheel
driving through bevel gears the vertical shaft on which other
bevel-wheels would turn the driving shafts, the tumbling

shafts, on each floor of the mill. This lease, which was for twenty-four years, was renewed and for some time the mill continued to be worked by Cockshutts as a cotton mill, but ceased before 1847 when it was noted by the Ordnance Survey as a cotton mill in ruins. A few years later it was pulled down and the stone was used to build the Ploughleys Barn in Malham West Field. All that now remain are the name Old Mill Foss and slight traces of the bridge and goit.

The story of these two mills is typical of many in the dales of Ribble, Aire and Wharfe, but in the more northerly dales, Wensleydale, Swaledale, and the smaller dales around Sedbergh, Dentdale, Garsdale and the Rawthey valley the last decade of the eighteenth century saw wool beginning to find an important place among the converted cornmills, through what was a traditional occupation, that of knitting stockings and caps. For generations the people of these dales had spun some of their wool into knitting yarns, and men, women and children had become habitual knitters. Markets for yarn and knitted goods were well established at Kendal and Richmond and great quantities of stockings were sent from them to London. Kendal, at the end of the eighteenth century, was reported as handling nearly 30,000 dozens of stockings a year. The local wool was spun into a fine knitting yarn, collected and then 'put out' for knitting by whole families. The knitted goods were collected by men known as 'stockingers' and carried from the dales to Kirkby Stephen or Kendal for transmission to London. In 1666, after the Kaber Rigg Plot in which men of the upper Wensleydale and Swaledale area, with those of part of Westmorland, plotted to restore the Commonwealth, one of the agents of the plotters was described at the trials as a 'stockinger of Askrigg'. Such a man, visiting the remote farmsteads carrying his pack of yarn or stockings and going regularly to the towns, would be an ideal agent, moving regularly through all the countryside without comment.

This background of traditional knitting was seen by some families already engaged in the wool dealing as a ready-made outlet for machine-spun yarns which could be made in some of the abandoned cornmills. Birkbecks of Settle, Dovers of the Sedbergh area, Knowles in Swaledale, all saw the possibilities and, from 1790 onwards, not only converted some cornmills but built a few new mills for yarn spinning. The existence of a well-established traditional industry gave the worsted-yarn spinning a local outlet for its product and also encouraged the development of weaving. In some of the new mills such materials as horse-cloths and plaids were woven and for a time the harder yarns were used in carpet weaving. The worsted mills remained active in the northern dales to a later date than did the cotton mills farther south.[2]

During the first half of the nineteenth century there was a gradual sorting out of the dales mills into areas of special trade, brought about in part by the developing transport facilities and the larger concentration of particular industries into defined areas. The completion of the Leeds and Liverpool Canal gave Skipton a direct and cheap through connexion with the cotton towns of Lancashire, and Skipton's closest connexions were with upper Airedale and Wharfedale, so these dales, along with lower Ribblesdale, became essentially cotton-spinning areas. The northern and north-western dales had their connexions with Richmond and Kendal, old centres of hand knitting, so these dales, Wensleydale, Swaledale, Dentdale and Garsdale, developed into a worsted- and knitting-yarn area with coarser yarn going to Barnard Castle for carpet weaving. Nidderdale became an area of flax spinning and hemp preparation, of considerable importance. When the flax industry was established in Leeds, several new mills, particularly in the Washburn valley and a few in Nidderdale, were built to take a part in this trade. Nidderdale had its older connexions with the great linen-weaving centre of Knaresborough.

Nearly all the mills which survived the middle nineteenth century had supplemented the water power with a steam-engine or had gone over entirely to steam drive. A few wheels survived to serve mills which changed to sawmills or other trades which made only moderate power demands. The cotton mills mostly ceased to work about 1850 and the industry left the dales for towns like Skipton, Gargrave and Settle.

Archdeacon Boyd makes a typical comment on Arncliffe Mill when speaking of the depopulation of the dales –

> this was less noticeable in Arncliffe, for the flour mill was transformed into a cotton mill about the year 1820 and this afforded for some years employment for the youngsters of the village at home . . . the whole thing had to be abandoned and since that time the population has considerably decreased.

What brought to an end the cotton mills, so numerous and widespread during the first half of the nineteenth century? A simple and satisfactory answer is difficult to find, as many factors were involved in the decline. The long transport of raw and finished goods and the distance from markets was an obvious disadvantage, and the small capital resources, with the small size of individual units, was another. A more serious factor, however, is inherent in the water-wheel itself and in some of its unique attributes. It has been estimated that many of the early cornmills had wheels which were little if any more than a single horsepower, just enough to turn a pair of stones. In the seventeenth century some of these small wheels were replaced by larger wheels, but as late as the eighteenth century they were only of low power and very inefficient.

The centuries of wear had borne heavily on mills and wheels, and repairs and patches may have replaced all the original structures, but little change or improvement had taken place in the basic design. In the richer corn country, with large placid rivers, mills had increased their power by building their wheels of greater and greater width, but the extra water demanded by these wheels was not available in our small upland streams and our rivers were too much subject to flood and drought to attract more than the very exceptional large mill. Occasionally, as at Linton Mill about 1790, a second dam was built right across the river, above the first, to impound a great length of deep water which could keep the mill going through most droughts, but this was the work of the wealthy Birbeck family, woollen and worsted merchants and bankers.

A changed situation was brought about when Smeaton, the Yorkshire engineer, designer of the Eddystone Lighthouse, turned his mind to the problem of the water-wheel as a source of power. In 1752 he worked with a model wheel of two-foot diameter, and after much very accurate experiment he determined the efficiency of different types of wheel and designed more efficient buckets and other details. He introduced cast iron for the shaft, and early in the nineteenth century he and other engineers were making most of the wheel of iron. To convert an old mill to greater efficiency and capacity, however, demanded a big capital outlay – a new wheel might cost a few hundred pounds, and a larger mill building, improved dam and goit, mill gear and machinery added to this financial burden which was usually beyond any local resources. Businessmen from the textile areas, bankers and merchants, formed small companies to improve and run the new mills, but only a few of the dales mills were suitable for this scale of investment.

The wheel itself had characteristics which limited its use. It is a gravity machine using the pull of gravity on water filling the buckets on one side of the wheel. The buckets are filled at the top and empty themselves near the bottom, travelling part of the circular track of the wheel's circumference. This brings the water in the buckets under the action of centrifugal force proportioned to the velocity of the wheel's rim, and when this force reaches a certain amount the water will fly out of the buckets and cease to turn the wheel. Because of this, a wheel can only turn up to a maximum speed which depends upon its diameter. It can soon be calculated that a wheel of 20-ft diameter begins to throw out the water from the buckets at a little above six revolutions per minute, and so to lose its power. As the diameter of the wheel increases, so the speed must be reduced, so that a 40-ft-diameter wheel could only run properly at about four revolutions per minute, and a 50-ft wheel at less than this.

Now processes like machine spinning needed high speeds on the machine; these were increased by successive improvements and inventions. Greater power was needed and was generally sought by means of a bigger wheel, but here there was an inevitable conflict. A larger-diameter wheel was slower, so more and more 'mill work', gear-wheels, etc, was necessary to keep the machinery running at the proper speed. This was expensive and more gears meant loss of power through friction. A wide wheel needed more water and the limit of capacity of the small streams was soon reached. It was these factors, due to the nature of the water-wheel, which put a final limit to its adaptability to an expanding industry. So long as a mill was small a wheel could serve, but expansion had to break away from these limitations and for the new source of power the steam-engine was necessary. The great quantity of coal consumed by these early engines, most of which had to be carried into the dales from the canal by long road haulages, created an additional burden of transport and cost beyond what the industry could carry. The cost of water was practically nil beyond a small water-rent charge, and it was put back into the stream to serve another and another mill as often as wanted. The coal was expensive and was burned to ashes and smoke.

The economic solution of these problems was to leave the dales and move to towns like Skipton where, in the first half of the nineteenth century, more and more steam-driven mills were built along the banks of the canal. Firms like Dewhirst gradually closed many small water-mills in the dales and concentrated all their work in their new mills in Skipton. Dales families followed them for employment, and the decline in dales population had set in.

Today, in many small valleys the ruins of mills can be traced, mainly recognizable by dam and goit leading to the pile of foundations. A few wheels remain but are becoming fewer every year as the electricity grid extends over the rural areas. Mill-wheels at Embsay, Gargrave, Slaidburn, Skyreholm, and other places, which a few years ago were happily turning and were noticed in the guidebooks and admired by visitors, are now either derelict or in most cases removed altogether, their place taken by the more adaptable electric motor. Of the few which remain, an all-iron wheel at Hartlington still powers the saw bench and lathes of a carpenter's and wood turner's shop; one at Wath in Nidderdale has stopped only within the last few months, and its fate still hangs in the balance. A wheel at the old cornmill in Skipton is being restored for preservation and it will certainly attract the interest of many visitors. Another wheel has been restored at Galphay and now operates a circular saw and a grindstone, this being only a 15-ft wheel, while at Darley in Nidderdale a small flax-spinning mill is still turned in part by a 20-ft wheel, reconditioned after serious breakages in 1953.

A large number of water-wheels were used on the mines, but

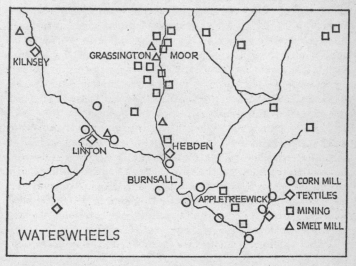

Fig 9. Water-wheels in a mining area. 8 miles of upper Wharfe-dale, *c* 1850

as most of these have been closed for nearly a century little now remains but the pits in which they ran, and more and more of these are now being filled in.[3] Soon there will be a generation to whom the water-wheel is only a sentimental idea figuring in old pictures and not a thing of actual experience, except perhaps in a folk museum and in an occasional rare example preserved for the small estate mill or by some really interested person. In their day they contributed much to the prosperity of the dales and served through an important early development stage of the textile industries, and their story should not be forgotten (Fig 9).

CHAPTER SEVEN

Haulage and transport

THE WHOLE of the Yorkshire dales has had experience of mining, either for lead or coal or in some places for copper, zinc or iron. There are true mining fields which stretch across large areas and where mining was everywhere a dominant occupation. There are two such fields, one includes practically all Swaledale above Marske with part of the north side of Wensleydale; the other lies west of upper Nidderdale, from within a mile or two west of Pateley Bridge, extending across the moors of Greenhow Hill and Appletreewick, then keeping on the north flank of Wharfedale, across Hebden, Grassington, Conistone and Kettlewell moors. This is a narrow field, only just over a mile from north to south but about twelve miles east to west. Almost all the area of these fields is scattered with the visible remains of mining; shafts and levels, mine-spoil heaps, buildings, watercourses and ruins which need interpretation but which can be put down with some confidence as the apparatus of some mining process or other. Outside these principal mining fields there are innumerable small veins and groups of veins in the limestones and coal seams in the Millstone Grits, so that isolated mines and mining trails are liable to be met with in nooks and corners of the fells, in remote valleys, or even on some of the 'tops' of high moor[1] (Illus. 16).

Much of the earliest mining was done by 'open cut', just digging out a vein at the surface, and traces of this kind of work remain as rather irregular trenches, grass-grown now, if not obscured by later work. Other work is marked by 'bell pits', a row of circular hollows, each surrounded by a bank of spoil and continuing along a vein like beads on a string. These were small working shafts, used one after another and abandoned in turn as they got to the limit of safe working. In these early forms of mining, ore and spoil could be lifted from the mine by a simple jack-roller, but in the sixteenth and seventeenth centuries, when mines were pushed down deeper, the weight of a longer rope soon became too much for the strength of a man at a jack-roller and lifting ore from the mine presented a new problem. Its solution has left a mark on the mining ground which is often seen but is sometimes the subject of speculation. This mark is the 'gin race' or 'whim track' (Illus. 17). The horse gin or, as it is sometimes called, the whim, was a simple but striking contrivance which changed little over the two centuries or more of its use. The essential part was a strong vertical shaft of timber, eight or nine feet long, shod with an iron foot which could run in a footstep bearing, usually of iron but sometimes of brass, let into a large rock. The top of the shaft, fitted with an iron running spike, was held vertical in the centre of a crossbeam which ran between two well-braced end posts, so that the shaft could rotate. This central shaft had at its upper end a 'barrel' or 'cage' on which the pit rope was wound, and lower than this a cross arm with provision at each end for fastening to it a set of horse harness. This cross arm would turn freely inside the end supports of the top beam. Now, with a horse harnessed at each end, they could move round in a circle, turning the central shaft and barrel and thus winding the two ends of the pit rope up and down the shaft, the ropes running over a couple of guide pulleys on a shaft-head 'poppet' (Fig 10). Such a two-horse whim was powerful enough for most deep shafts and could lift ore and spoil, or if necessary bring up kibbles (large iron buckets) of water and drain the mine.

The whims came into general use in the north in the eighteenth century and we can gather a few details about them from various contemporary sources. In the Durham coalfield, where Newcomen steam-engines were being introduced for colliery pumping, occasional trials were made to demonstrate the advantages of the new methods of drainage, both in performance and cost. The trials are usually recorded in the following form: 'Estimate of the Difference of the Expence in Drawing Water by Fire Engine & Drawing it by Horses, made Dec. 11, 1752'. Such is the title of a long and detailed account, but the relevant point for us is that the whim was operated by two horses for three hours, and then another pair took their place, the horses working through twenty-four hours of day and night in eight shifts of three hours. The minimum number of horses was six to work the twenty-four hours, though eight were better. This, of course, was for lifting water, which was a continuous process. For ore lifting the work was intermittent and was usually confined to the single working-day period, and with this probably two horses could cope.

Fig 10. Whim or gin for two ponies

One mine in the dales, owned by the Coalgrove Head Company and situated on Grassington Moor, found the mine to be a good one and worked deeper, so that the jack-roller became of little use. In October 1755 they wrote to William Brown, a Newcastle 'viewer'.[2] In the eighteenth century the 'viewer' in the northern coalfield was what we should call a mining engineer and consultant. He made surveys of collieries and advised on problems, and sometimes, as was the case with Brown, would act as agent to procure a steam-engine or machinery and would supervise its instalment and be on hand for maintenance problems as well. Brown was one of the best known of the eighteenth-century viewers and had worked in Tyneside, Cumberland and other fields.

He was asked to design and supply a whim suitable for the

draining of Coalgrove Head mine and his letters give a good idea of the dimensions and building of a typical, though fairly large whim. The fact that Brown was brought from Newcastle suggests that whims were something new and not yet in use in this part of Yorkshire. John Robinson, agent for the mine, wrote to Brown saying that his partnership thought it best if they supplied the required timbers and Brown got the necessary ironwork, so they ask what sizes of timber are wanted. Can Brown 'do with oak poles instead of fir, fir being at a great Distance from the place and must consequently come very dear'. Brown replies

he cannot well use oak instead of fir for four of the longest poles. The Longest, Strongest and best of the Poles which we call Overtree must be nothing less than Sixty foot long and about 9 or 10 inches square. The other three is what we call Cross tree and wings must be one of them near 40 foot long & 2 about 36 foot long each – they are what we call Long Ussers and will square near 9 inch at thick end and not more than 5 inch at small end. Oak is by much the best for all other things required to be made of Wood.

Brown would like to send over his own enginewright to choose the timber and to consider how he is to get the long piece of fir. He can have all the ironwork made at $3\frac{1}{2}d$ ($1\frac{1}{2}$p) a pound in Newcastle. He wants to know where the place is that the engines are to be erected with the right road thereto. The wright was to be sent to Richmond, from where Robinson would direct him. In January 1756 Robinson tells Brown that

the roads are so Excessive Rotten that it will be difficult to get Timber and other Materials Led till they be better. I say for the above Reason it will be better to defer Erecting the Engine till Aprill or May when one may hope the Weather and Roads will be much better.

The Lancashire carriers from Newcastle are recommended as coming through Richmond on the direct road through Grassington. It is not easy to see which route this would be – possibly by Wensley and Coverdale, from Richmond, coming down into Kettlewell and so down dale. This was certainly a road in use in the eighteenth century; the alternative was by Ripon and Pateley Bridge, though this could more profitably have avoided a call at Richmond. The distance is about 100 miles.

When this whim was finally erected it had a circular track for the horses of 40 ft diameter, well paved with gravel-sized spoil from the mine, and a central block of sandstone about 5 ft by 4 ft which carried the footstep bearing. Traces of these can still be seen.

The later story of this mine shows some of the stages in development which affected many of the larger mines in the northern fields. As the mine proved rich and workings were taken to greater depths, lifting water by kibbles and whim became too slow and pumps were a necessity. To work these continuously a water-wheel was built, but water could only be brought from a distant stream to a suitable place where a small dam could be made, at a point nearly half a mile away from the mineshaft. The dam was built and a water-wheel was set up, its power being transmitted to Coalgrove Head mine by means of wooden rods.

The rods were suspended in chains just clear of the ground and any natural obstacles, and were held up by timber tripods. A crank on the wheel axle moved them back and forth. The line of rods was 680 yds long and at 400 yds there is the trace of a 'bob pit' where a V-shaped bob was included in the line of rods, to cut out some of the sideways 'whip'. At the shaft head the rods moved a bell-crank (L-shaped) lever to translate the horizontal to vertical movement and so operate pump rods in the shaft. When the 'rod engine' was at last working, the large whim became the ore winder, taking over from a smaller one, not now strong enough for the work.

A deep drainage level, the Duke's Level, driven under the moor, reached the workings of the Coalgrove Head mine soon after 1824 and then the rods and pumps only lifted water from such workings as were sunk below the Duke's Level, to deliver it into that drain. As the mines extended, winding by whims became less and less efficient as the time for each deeper wind became longer, and a new system was designed, probably by John Taylor, the Cornish mining engineer, who in 1818 became mineral agent to the Duke of Devonshire. In this scheme the main points were, briefly, the sinking or deepening of a few shafts at selected positions and their interconnexion underground; the construction of a new system of watercourses to bring water for wheels both for winding and ore dressing; and a system of roads for overground transport. The old Coalgrove Head 'engine-wheel' was taken down and a new wheel, 45 ft in diameter and 6 ft wide was put in at the high winding-house, not far from the engine-wheel site (the pit is still there), which wound the Coalgrove Head shaft and also had a stronger set of pump rods alongside the rope. A little lower down the moor another and larger wheel, 52 ft by 6 ft, the brake-house wheel, wound four of the new shafts, with a total of 4,480 yds of wire rope. Whims were still used at the shafts not included in this reconstruction.[3]

At the Low Moor, better known as Yarnbury, a complex system was evolved which is worth looking at as remains of it are still to be seen. The workings on a complex group of east to west veins were taken deeper, so that a 50-fathom level connected them with a branch of the Duke's Level for drainage. The main working levels were at 20 fathoms and 35 fathoms depth, and there were four main shafts. A deep shaft, Mason's, was sunk and a north to south crosscut level driven right across the Yarnbury veins at 35 fathoms, thus connecting all workings at that depth. A second shaft, Barrett's, drove a crosscut parallel to Mason's but at 20 fathoms, and at several places short internal shafts or inclines were made for easy movement from the 35- to the 20-fathom system. The 20-fathom network was wound by a large whim at Barrett's and the 35-fathom at Mason's. Two other shafts, Tomkin's and Bowden's, also did some winding from both (Fig 11).

For movement in the 20-fathom network, ponies were later used to pull the tubs and for their descent into the mine an incline was made from the surface near Mason's shaft to cut the 20-fathom network about 100 yds away and not far from

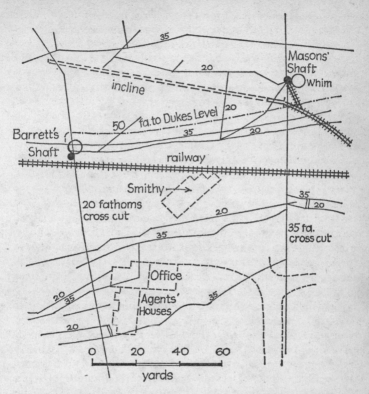

Fig 11. Underground and winding arrangements at Yarnbury mines, lines with numbers are levels and depth in fathoms

Barrett's shaft. The portal of the incline, in beautifully-cut masonry, has the date 1827.

New dressing floors were built some distance from Mason's shaft, near a dam which could power the water-wheels for stamps and dressing machinery, and Mason's, Barrett's and Tomkin's shafts were connected to the floors by a railway. This had stone sleepers, stone blocks about 12 ins by 18 ins which each carry two peg holes for securing a chair, and which are set to a gauge of 42 ins and at about yard intervals along the line. Such fragments of rail as remain show a bullhead section and are 'fish-bellied', but unfortunately none of the wheels or trucks have been found and it is unlikely that any survive. This form of railway was also used in some others of the larger dressing floors and mines, and Taylor, reporting in 1831, says:

> The transport in various directions of large masses of stuff used to be attended by considerable charges; these are now much reduced, not only by the means that the railways themselves afford, but also in many cases from improvements in the arrangement of the different processes on the dressing floors, which have been suggested by the use of railroads, and which have made important alterations by avoiding that handling backwards and forwards which was too much the former practice, and which of itself occasioned considerable expense. One of the best instances of arrangements of this sort, connected by well-constructed railroads, is to be seen at the mines belonging to the Duke of Devonshire at Grassington, which reflects much credit upon Captain Barratt, the resident agent, who has laid out the most systematic plan of ore-dressing that I know of.

Among some ideas which were tried out, Mr Flint, the agent who started the Duke's Level in 1796 at Grassington, intended to make this serve as a boat level or canal (Illus. 19). For this purpose it was to be driven 9 ft high and 5 ft wide, and was to be a smaller pattern based upon the Nent Force Level then being driven in Alston Moor. However, when Taylor came he reduced these dimensions to those of an ordinary drainage level, on the ground that if it were completed the cost of bringing the ore to the mines from the mouth of the level in Hebden Gill would be greater than winding it to the moor, and a large new dressing floor would have to be built in the gill, much farther away from the smelt mill than the existing floors. The idea of a canal level, however, was applied in a Swaledale mine in 1820. The Blakethwaite vein, which had proved rich in the moors at

1. Halton Gill at the head of Littondale

2. Ingleborough from the south-west

3. Limestone pavement above Malham Cove, at the head of Airedale

4. The head of Swaledale from the Buttertubs Pass

5. Upper Swaledale from near Low Row

6. Dentdale and Howgill Fells

7. Wensleydale near Redmire and Bolton Castle

8. Wensleydale near Hawes. Small farms with meadow and pasture

9. Gunnerside, a Norse hamlet expanded to eighteenth-century mining village

10. A farmer's lime kiln

11. Kettlewell. Fells rising to Great Whernside

12. Conistone. Kilnsey Crag and the mouth of Littondale across the valley. Village school (closed) at right foreground

13. Modern lime kilns, Skyrethorns

14. Intakes on the side of Calver, near Reeth, Swaledale. Healaugh in the valley bottom

15. Low Mill, Grassington. Smelt-mill foundations to left of stream

16. Mining ground along Middle Vein, Grassington Moor

17. A 'gin race' on the Grassington Moor mines

18. Water-wheel at Foster Beck flax mill, near Pateley

19. The entrance to Duke's Level, Hebden Gill

20. Cam road along which Torrington travelled. A drove road, Ingleborough in the background

21. Penygent and the farm Dale Head, a meeting-place of packmen.
Several green roads converge here at Ulfkill Cross. The Pennine Way
goes through Dale Head . . . and along the summit of Penygent

22. Attermire Scar on the Mid Craven Fault. It was excavations in the numerous caves of these scars that inspired the Wharfedale archaeologists

23. Broad Scar, Malham Moor. Tarn House in the woods in the background

24. Halton Gill School (1626)

25. The smelt-mill chimney, Malham Moor

26. Pateley Bridge, Nidderdale

27. Threshfield grammar school (1674)

the head of Gunnerside Gill, was proved farther to the east and was worked as the Bishop vein from the Bishop shaft and one at the head of Little Punchard Gill. A quarter of a mile north of this vein was another, the Cocker vein, with two shafts on it. The workings of both mines were troubled with water and the road from the mines to the smelt mills was a rough track over wild and high moorlands, Bishop's shaft being at 1,800 ft OD. To unwater the mines and give a better access, Stone's Level was driven from a point about 1,350 ft OD in Little Punchard Gill, and after cutting the Cocker vein it was continued until it reached the Bishop vein. The mouth of this level was walled to convert it into a canal, waygates were cut into the Cocker and Bishop workings for loading places, and ore was boated out of the mine. An easier road was made from this level mouth to the smelt mills in Arkengarthdale, and for some years the scheme was very successful.

Inclines were also occasionally used. In Swaledale one of the most important veins worked by the Old Gang companies was the Friarfold. The principal drawing level for this and other veins was the Hard Level, driven from a point nearly 1¼ miles south of the Friarfold. About a quarter of a mile south of the Friarfold there is a smaller vein, the Brandy Bottle, the origin of the name being now forgotten. To get access to this vein from the surface, Bell's shaft was sunk where Black's crosscut intersected it from part of the Old Gang workings. Two parallel inclines were brought down from the surface almost over the line of the crosscut. Hall, who drove the inclines, was agent at the Old Gang between 1811 and 1818, so this dates the work. Hall planned to use a steam-engine to haul Friarfold ore to the surface up these inclines, but the engine was never installed, probably because of the difficulty of getting adequate coal supplies, and for some years the inclines were only used as access ways for horses for underground haulage; the ore was wound by Bell's and Williams' shafts and carried overground to the Old Gang smelt mill. In the mid-nineteenth century a whim was erected at the mouth of one incline and ore was hauled up it as originally intended. From points along the incline three levels were driven to open up other vein workings.

The mechanical problems we have just discussed all arose in and around the mines, but as they were solved and production increased a much wider problem was created – that of the carriage of lead from the mines and of stores and coal to them. Smelt mills were in general fairly close to the mines and it was the custom of most fields that the miners should deliver their ore, properly dressed, at the smelt mill. For the miner on a small mine this was not a serious demand as his quantities were small, his parcels of ore not much more than a ton at once, and a normal string of pack ponies could deal with it in one journey. On most fields there were carriers, like Joseph Calvert of Bewerley, who gave evidence in an Exchequer deposition in 1750 'that he kept a set of carriage horses (packhorses) for the carriage of lead and servants for that purpose' and that he was employed to carry pigs of lead from Yarnbury to Pateley Bridge. There were some roads on which carts could be used, but these were mainly east of Ripon and Richmond and across the lower ground of the Pennine foothills and the Vale of York. As early as 1365, 24 fothers (about 21 cwt to the fother) of lead were sent from Greenhow near Pateley Bridge to Boroughbridge by 'two waggons, each with 10 oxen . . . by high and rocky mountains and by muddy roads', about 20 leagues and this occupied 24 days (more than one journey, of course).

We have seen in Robinson's letter to Brown that winter travel was difficult for large objects, and in fact there would be little movement except by the packhorses which could pick their way and were not so closely dependent upon a road as was a waggon. We may, however, remind ourselves of the quantity of traffic of which we are thinking. On Grassington Moor the output, which in 1750 was just over 400 tons of smelted lead, thanks to some of the improvements we have looked at, had risen by 1760 to just over 600 tons a year. All this meant a much greater weight of ore and rock to be lifted from the mines by horse whims, dressed, and then carried to the smelt mill. As smelted lead some of it was carried to Pateley Bridge and some to Skipton for sale.

The packhorses carried between $2\frac{1}{4}$ and $2\frac{1}{2}$ cwt each load,

that is eight or nine horses for each ton carried. The 600 tons
of lead thus mean about 5,400 horse-loads of lead and not less
than 7,000 horse-loads of ore at the pre-smelt mill stage. The
smelting was done with coal brought from collieries on
Threshfield Moor and Thorpe Fell, three or four miles away.
Again some 4,000 horse-loads were needed. Stores, timber,
rails and so on were to be carried from woods and foundries,
so we shall not be overstating the case if we reckon that in and
about the mines and the ten miles of roads to Skipton,
Gargrave and Pateley Bridge, something between 16,000 and
20,000 horse-loads were carried in a normal year. The horses
and their drivers must have been a major feature of the life of
the area. Some people like Calvert kept ten or twenty horses, a
'set', and were in fact regular carriers. Most of the local farmers
kept one or two horses on hire to the mines and some of the
mine partnerships had their one or two horses for the whim
which, when not winding, could deal with the carriage of ore to
the smelt mill.

This was becoming an unmanageable problem; finding,
feeding and tending the number of horses required was beyond
the capacity of the area and new methods of transport were
essential. This was not a problem which had grown slowly by
unnoticed increments. In the year 1701–2 Grassington mines
had their old smelt mill on the riverside, near Linton Church,
equipped with two ore hearths. The principal fuel was 'chop
wood'. This was wood cut to suitable size and length, barked
and dried in a kiln until all the sap was got rid of. Along with
this a small amount of coal was used. Now in this year May
1701 to May 1702 the mill smelted 79 fother and 3 pieces of
lead, ie, just over 87 tons, and for this the following fuel was
used:

from Grass Wood (1½ miles)	185 loads of chopwood
from Bolton Parks (9 miles)	432 loads of chopwood
from Thorpe Colliery (2 miles)	97 loads of coal

A small number of horses could easily manage this modest
transport. The expansion of mining on Grassington Moor really

began about 1730 when the 'free miners' were forming their partnerships and output rose to around 150 tons of smelted lead in the year. By 1745 it had risen to 400 tons and by 1760 was 600 tons in a good year. The horse-transport problem was now of serious dimensions, as we have noted earlier, for the single area of Grassington Moor. Multiply this by the number of comparable areas in the dales and it becomes obvious that a new solution had to be found. This was provided by the substitution of roads of sufficient quality to carry carts and waggons in winter as well as in summer, and adequate provision for their maintenance.

In the 1750s turnpike trusts were being formed and their roads were being built at a great rate in Yorkshire, mainly between the market towns which were linked with the woollen industry. The Keighley to Kendal turnpike was built through Skipton in 1753 as a link between the wool-growing areas around Kendal and the wool market of Halifax, already linked by a good road with Keighley. In a broadsheet in favour of this road it is said

> Good Roads would lower the Price of Coal at least one-Third ... When the Roads are effectually repaired Goods may be conveyed from one Place to another in Carriages with less than Half the Number of Horses now employed in carrying Packs and consequently at half the Expence.

The example of the Keighley and Kendal turnpike was not lost upon the many investors in the Grassington mine partnerships. These included several merchants and traders in Pateley Bridge, Ripon and Knaresborough, as well as such people as Henry Alcock; Henry Wickham, JP; P. W. Overend, JP; and others, who were also trustees at one time or another of the Keighley and Kendal turnpike and other roads in the Skipton district. It is thus not surprising that in 1758, when the lead output from the moor was still increasing, they should promote the Grassington, Pateley and Wetherby road and thus create a connexion to Hull where lead could be shipped for London.[4] An Act was obtained in May 1758 'for repairing and widening the road leading from Wetherby ... through Knaresborough, Ripley ... Pateley Bridge, Greenhaugh Hill and Hebden, to Grassington'. By a later Amending and Continuing Act the Grassington to Pateley Bridge section was separated from the other. This part of the road served almost entirely the market traffic for Pateley Bridge and Grassington, which were the principal miners' markets.

A large proportion of the promoters of this Act, who loaned money for the project, were partners in mines at Grassington or Greenhow, some of them active miners and others investors in partnerships which used a group of local men to operate their mines. The money was raised by subscriptions in various sums, from £20 to the largest, from Mr Henry Alcock, £385. Alcock was an investor in several of the Grassington mines and was also a partner with Birbeck of Settle in the bank soon to become the Craven Bank of Skipton, where he was in a good practice as a lawyer. The road was built with a toll bar at Craven Cross on Greenhow Hill, near the boundary between Craven and Nidderdale. After the first run of twenty-one years, Continuing Acts were passed from time to time, but these only applied to the separated portion, Grassington to Pateley Bridge.

The expenses of the road were not very great and the income from letting tolls was sufficient to cover day-to-day repairs and the interest on loans. The trustees, however, found it difficult to repay their loans on short term and had to renew their powers to borrow in each Continuing Act. The expenses accounts are very formal and dull and have only one or two items worth notice. In January 1787 they

Pd. Wm. Tomlin for Cutting and Dressing,
   Lettering and Setting etc. Milestones
   from Pateley Bridge to Grassington   £3 9 0

There are ten milestones, all to one pattern – triangular pillars of fine sandstone, 11 ins wide and standing 27 ins above ground, lettered on two sides, eg, P 6M and G 4M. There were constant small repairs at the turnpike bar house at Craven Cross, but in 1790 and 1791 there seems to have been damage at the gate:

1790 Aug 7	Pd. Mr Lellon for a large new Lock for the Gate at Craven Cross	8	0
	Pd. John West for setting on Lock and repairing the Gate and Turnstile	2	0
1791 Mch 5	Pd. John Milward for new leading and Glazing the Windows at Turnpike House	13	0
June 25	John West for making a new Gate at Craven Cross	7	6
	John Birch for Bolts for do and for repairs at Turn Stile	4	6

For a time the road caused a reorientation of Grassington and upper Wharfedale interests from Skipton towards Pateley and Ripon. For much of its earlier history Wharfedale had been linked with Skipton, both through the large estates of the Cliffords of Skipton Castle and by the old market road between Skipton, Grassington and Kettlewell which continued over Coverdale to Leyburn and Richmond. As the arable agriculture declined in the dales, its place was taken by the growth of corn markets in Skipton and the change over to cattle-rearing and feeding in the dales, with corn bought there. More and more land on the eastern flank of the Pennines, in particular the Knaresborough Forest and the Vale of York, was turning to corn production, and when the Grassington to Pateley Bridge, Ripley and Knaresborough road was completed it was easier for the corn to come direct to Pateley and Grassington markets by this road as a return load in the lead carts than to bring it up from Skipton. Also several of the Knaresborough and Pateley Bridge merchants were investors in the mines and seized the chance to extend their merchanting trade into these markets. In the valley of the little River Dibb, in the upper part of Appletreewick township, the Aket Colliery was opened out and was able, on this road, to send coal both to Grassington and to Greenbow Hill for the smelt mills. The Appletreewick

mines were in the royalty of Yorke of Bewerley, adjoining
Pateley Bridge, so these mines were also brought into the
Pateley Bridge orbit, their ore being carried to Heathfield smelt
mill near Pateley.

This diversion of upper Wharfedale interests into Nidderdale was not to become permanent, and the factor which
eventually returned interest to Skipton was the Leeds and
Liverpool Canal. This was completed from Leeds to Holme
Bridge, Gargrave, by 1777 and in the next few years it became
an important trading concern with warehouses at Gargrave and
Skipton and with coal and stone wharves at both places. The
tolls levied on the Grassington to Pateley Bridge turnpike
show the preoccupation with the movement of coal by their
very easy terms. Tolls to be paid at Craven Cross Bar:

	s	d
One horse		$1\frac{1}{2}$
One horse cart		6
Two horse cart	1	$1\frac{1}{2}$
Three horse cart	1	6
Four horse waggon	1	$10\frac{1}{2}$
Four horse chaise	1	$10\frac{1}{2}$
One horse coal cart		1
Two horse coal cart		3
Four horse coal cart		6
Cattle, one score		10
Sheep and pigs		5

Most of the coal, however, was moved to the various smelt
mills and not much that could be called house coal was
produced. By about 1790, when the coal pits were becoming
troubled with water, the Duke of Devonshire's agents at
Grassington turned to the canal as a source of better-quality
coal in greater quantity. The road from Grassington to
Gargrave ran for much of its way through manors belonging
to the Duke, and he was able to promote its improvement
without the necessity for a turnpike trust. This better coal was
brought to Grassington, but much was sent along the Pateley

road to the mills on Greenhow Hill, and from some intermediate areas, like Burhills and others in the Appletreewick
royalties, miners sent ore to Grassington for smelting, thus
keeping this road open, but for reduced through traffic.

With this reorientation and effectual shortening of the
Pateley road, and also with the great increase in cattle-dealing,
the old road to Skipton became busy again; Skipton market
took precedence over Pateley and Ripon, and Grassington and
Kettlewell markets ended. The final effect of all this was that
in 1853 the road from Cracoe to Skipton, part of the old road
from Grassington, was realigned and made into a turnpike
and the Gargrave road was left more or less as a country lane.
Coal, lead, corn and cattle were now concentrated at the
Skipton wharves and market and although the Gargrave
wharf was kept on for a certain amount of Lancashire trade
upper Wharfedale was once more vitally connected with
Skipton.

With this new connexion, or rather re-connexion, and when
the railway reached Skipton in 1845, schemes for railways to
serve the dales were produced but not implemented. The
Wharfedale Railway Company reported opposition in 1845,
but the Skipton and Wharfedale Railway Act was passed in
1865. In 1882, although the railway had not been built, an
Amending Act to extend the powers granted to carry the line
by Kettlewell and through Wensleydale to Darlington was
sought. Another Act was obtained in 1908 for the Upper
Wharfedale Light Railway (Grassington, Kettlewell and
Buckden) as an extension to the Yorkshire Dales Railway
which had been built from Skipton to Grassington and
opened in 1902. Other proposals were for the Skipton and
Kettlewell Railway Company and the Skipton and North
Eastern Junction Railway. Of all of them, only the Yorkshire
Dales Railway was built as far as Grassington (Threshfield)
and that had barely a thirty-year life as a passenger line, then
settled down to its present status as a goods line only.

CHAPTER EIGHT

Cattle fairs, drovers, and packmen

IN 1792 Lord Torrington was crossing the dales from Askrigg to Ingleton and used what was then the common road for this journey. He could travel much of the way along the Roman road from Bainbridge, up Cam Fell, over the head of Duerley Dale, and then by the flank of Dodd Fell down to the ford across the Ribble not far from its source (Illus. 20). We can read some details of this journey in his diary where he makes the following comments:

I was much fatigued by the tediousness of the road where we met two farming men, with whom we conversed about the grouse, and their abundance. Crossing a ford, Mr Blakey led me to a public house – called Grierstones (Gearstones), the seat of misery, in a desert; and tho' filled with company, yet the Scotch fair held upon the heath added to the horror of the curious scenery: the ground in front crowded by Scotch cattle and the drovers; and the house cramm'd by the buyers and sellers most of whom were in plaids, fillibegs, etc. The stable did not afford hay. The only custom of this hotel or rather hovel, is derived from the grouse shooters, or from two Scotch Fairs; when at the conclusion of the days squabble the two Nations agree in mutual drunkenness, the Scotch are always wrap'd up in their plaids – as a defence against heat, cold or wet; but they are preventions of speed or activity: so whenever any cattle stray'd, they instantly threw down the plaid, that they might overtake them. All the Yorkshire around, tho' black and frightful seems of small account in the comparison of Ingleborough – at whose base we now travel.

At Ingleton he adds a note 'I saw vast droves of Scottish cattle passing to the South'.

In these comments we have the elements of a trade and its people, now vanished, which during the eighteenth century and overlapping from the seventeenth and to the early part of the nineteenth century, had populated roads and inns now almost forgotten or completely vanished, and which brought into the dales a way of life that now would appear completely alien. Against these comments of Lord Torrington we can set three events which have passed into an almost legendary history but which have a few common elements relevant to the subject of this chapter. They are like so many of the events of folk-lore and folk-memory, stories of violence which upset the normal uneventful life of the people – stories of the murder of strangers. These stories are located around the Hollow Mill Cross at the head of Swaledale, around a now-forgotten inn at Dead Man Hill, at the head of Nidderdale, and at the now ruined Waste Inn on Boss Moor at the head of the Winterburn valley. They take place in very remote places and involve people, not natives of the place, but still not entire strangers – people who are known as intermittent visitors on business – packmen and drovers.

Without going into great detail let us see what are the elements of these three stories before we discuss their relevance to our subject. It is more than coincidence that all three events are located not only in the 'waste' but at points on boundaries. The Waste Inn, though within the township of Rilston, is within thirty yards of the boundary with the adjoining township of Bordley and not much more from Threshfield. It is also within a few hundred yards of the watershed between Airedale and Wharfedale. Dead Man Hill is similarly near the watershed between Nidderdale and Coverdale, to a boundary between separate townships, and between the North and West Ridings. At Hollow Mill Cross Yorkshire and Westmorland meet between Eden and Swale, on the watershed between the Irish and North Seas.

Many of the inns, meeting-places and resting-places of drovers and packmen were so placed, the remote boundaries

being areas where the power and vigilance of the parish
constables was least felt and where tax- and toll-collectors were
least likely to come. There was little interference in these
places with gatherings either for pleasure or for business. A
lonely burial could be made in secrecy with little expectation of
subsequent discovery and with the maximum difficulty of
tracing the people who might have taken part. Two of the
people involved in these stories were packmen and one a
drover.

The Nidderdale story centres upon a small inn or alehouse at
Lodge, which was alongside a well-used packhorse way coming
over from Coverdale, climbing up Arkleside and crossing over
a rather wild top or moor. The inn was kept by a woman and
her daughter, and it was used year after year by a group of
Scots pedlars who called there on their seasonal visits. It was
noticed that three of the regular customers stopped calling and
their companions knew nothing of the reason. After a time the
wives of the men came seeking information but could gather
nothing. The township books of Middlesmoor, in which township the inn lay, have an entry '30 May 1728. three murder'd
Bodies were found burr'd on Lodge End without heads'. It
was assumed that these were the missing men and that they
had been murdered by the woman and her daughter at the inn.
It became a tradition in the dale that an unusual number of
Scottish ponies were to be seen on the neighbouring farms and
that many dales women were wearing Paisley shawls. The story
grew, and in time the hill where the inn stood was called Dead
Man Hill, the name it still bears. Needless to say the versions
of this story which are nearest our own time are the more
romantic ones.

The Boss Moor story is much more confused. A fair there
was at its height in the mid-eighteenth century, and from these
gatherings many stories were collected of the wild Scots
drovers, no doubt being edited and elaborated over the years.
The Waste Inn which served these drovers was the centre of
many stories of wild nights and of fights, and when in the
nineteenth century the skeletons of more than one man were
found on the moor, one of them under a large rock, the stories

changed from rumour and soon had details attached of the murder and robbery of rich drovers at the inn. These stories rest, however, only on almost forgotten legend and were probably inspired by the finding of bones which may have been of almost any age.

The Hollow Mill Cross murder is more completely documented and its significance is mainly political. On this wild borderland of Yorkshire and Westmorland there was established the secret and hidden headquarters of a group of Commonwealth supporters of the Kaber Rigg Plot of 1664. John Atkinson was a 'stockinger and Anabaptist', a small trader who travelled the dales as a packman and pedlar, collecting knitted goods for the Kendal and Kirkby Stephen markets. With this occupation and his regular journeys through the dales and over a wider country he made an ideal agent for the plotters. Atkinson was caught and hanged at Appleby along with others. The day after the hangings another pedlar, John Smith, was going from Thwaite in Swaledale over Birkdale by the Hollow Mill Cross to Kirkby Stephen, when he was set upon and murdered. The evidence which was collected was very confused; there were stories of two men being seen in the mist and a man seeking a horse near the Cross. The two men were said to be carrying something like a bundle of clothes, and at the same place some time later the corpse of a man was found in the peat. Conflicting stories soon grew up, some connecting Smith with the capture of Atkinson, many explaining the event as the robbery of a packman for his goods and money. The case was never finally determined.

It would be possible from these stories of the murder of packmen in lonely places to build up an imaginative picture of a wild life and of habitual violence along these ancient ways, but if a balanced view is taken the very opposite will be seen to be true. With the many thousands of people whose whole lives were spent travelling along these roads over some of the wildest country in England, carrying valuable goods, having on them large sums of money – sometimes very large after a successful selling – to find in a period of more than two centuries only three stories of violence and only one of them connected, and by popular report only, with robbery and that without positive evidence, we feel that we are glimpsing a people who might be rough in their manners but with whom honesty was a marked part of their character. If robbery and violence had been as much a part of their life as it was along the king's highways and in the towns, the droving and peddling trades could not have existed.

The roads and tracks used by these people form a close network over the high ground of the Pennines and deserve more careful study than they have so far been afforded. Many of these tracks are now seen in part as green lanes, but by far the greater lengths of them are now only bridleways, often obscure and recognized mainly on the sections which cross the high fells. Any student of them will soon become aware that there is a double pattern, two groups of roads superposed, differing in many details. For clarity it is necessary to separate these groups and to define some of their characteristic features. The older group of tracks, which also persisted in use to more recent times, is that of the roads linking up important medieval markets; in their course they pass through and serve many villages and hamlets. The best known of these roads are roughly cross-Pennine, connecting markets on the east and west flanks of this great barrier of moors and mountain (Fig 12).

Markets became necessary where great numbers of folk were settled who were occupied in other than food-producing work. Around the Norman castles armies of retainers, artificers, craftsmen and soldiers were to be fed, and the tastes of the Norman barons demanded wines, spices and other commodities which could not be produced locally. It was essential to have a market to which merchants could bring regular supplies and to which the surrounding villages could send their small surplus for sale. As the population increased, villages found their first common fields inadequate for their needs until more ground was cleared and brought into cultivation, and they, too, turned to the larger markets. All this brought into existence a traffic to and from the market towns which, in the early centuries after the Norman settlement, were few in number.

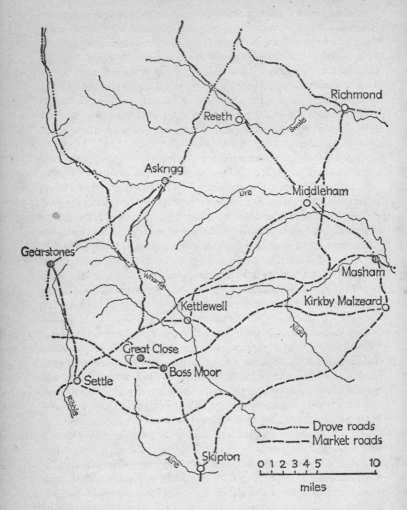

Fig 12. Drove roads and market roads across the dales

Within a few years of the Conquest the great Honour of Richmond had been created, stretching across the Pennines to the borders of Lancashire and from Wensleydale to Teesdale, with its garrison and centre at Richmond in Swaledale. The demands of this whole area centred upon Richmond, where a market was soon established and where merchants and crafts-men settled in numbers. Changes were felt, however, in the fifteenth century and a commission reporting in 1440 gave a very concise account of them.

... The town consisted of many burgesses, wealthy merchants, artificers, victuallers and other substantial in-habitants so that many strangers, merchants and others were wont to resort thither from Lancashire, Cumberland, and Westmorland, with merchandise of grain, victual and other goods, every Saturday in the year as well as conveyors and carryers of grain and bread belonging to (these) along with Lonsdale, Craven, Dent and Sedbergh in which no great quantity of corn was then grown, for which the inhabitants of those parts made their chief provision of grain in Richmond market ...

Complaint is made that, whereas the town formerly collected a hundred shillings a year in tolls, this was now changed because toll-free markets had been granted at Masham, Bedale and Middleton, and these, with Barnard Castle, were taking the traders; also because large tracts of waste had been brought into cultivation in the west parts and merchants from those parts now went to the free markets.

In fact, a similar but smaller challenge had been experienced in the thirteenth century, when many smaller markets were granted to convenient villages along the main market roads to Richmond. The tolls levied at Richmond market show some groups of merchant goods that could not come into the smaller markets, but which could compete with grain, wool, cloth, cheese, hides and butter. A more exotic group at Richmond is wines, fish, silk, lampreys, garlic and woad. Salt, wood, faggots, iron, lead and coal also were not likely to find a place in the village market. Markets comparable to Richmond had been established near the castles of Knaresborough, Kirkby Malzeard, Skipton, Kendal and Lancaster and other seats of the greater barons, and remarkably direct roads were soon formed between them. The villages through which these roads passed flourished more than their neighbours, as they benefited by the passage of goods and merchants between the larger markets which thus increased their resources.

A few customary markets in the dales have their origin in special circumstances. In the west part of the dales and over much of the Pennine watershed there was forest, which at the Conquest was granted to the Norman barons. At the heads of Swaledale and Wensleydale there were the forests of Swaledale, Mallerstang and Wensley, held by the Earl of Richmond. At the head of Wharfedale the forest of Litton and Langstrath was held by Percy, Earl of Northumberland. There were no villages within these forests, but foresters and forest servants inhabited many lodges and made up a moderate population not in a position to grow their own food. To meet their requirements markets were soon established in the nearest villages to the forest boundary – Reeth in Swaledale, Askrigg in Wensleydale, and Kettlewell in Wharfedale. Sooner or later these customary markets were regularized by charters, though in the case of Askrigg this was not until 1587.

Of these, Kettlewell was on a direct route between Settle and Kirkby Malzeard markets. A green road climbs out of Settle on to Langcliffe but is now lost in the modernized road as far as the crossing of the ancient road from Helwith Bridge across Malham Moor which the monks of Fountains refer to as early as 1206 as the 'road from Lonsdale'. Across this road a bridleway continues the road from Settle with unchanged direction, across the spur of Fountains Fell called Knowe Fell, and so to the modernized road down into Arncliffe in Litton-dale. Over Old Cote Moor into Wharfedale it has two branches. One goes to Kettlewell, then by a bridleway across Conistone Moor where it is called Sandgate, by Middlesmoor in Nidder-dale and so to Kirkby Malzeard and Masham. The other branch goes down to cross the Wharfe at Starbotton, and then

over between Great and Little Whernside into the head of
Nidderdale and on to Kirkby Malzeard, with a branch above
Kettlewell down Coverdale to Middleham and Richmond.
When a bridge was destroyed by flood in Kettlewell it was said
in Quarter Sessions' reports that 'packmen from Lancashire
are detained'. These were some of the market traders from
Lancaster, via Settle. Very little of this road could be used by
carts, so, as wheeled traffic developed, new lines along lower
country and through different villages were made and the
'market road' became only an upland bridleway.

The directness of the market roads was only possible because they were used by pack ponies, in ones and twos, or
possibly in trains or 'gangs' of up to twenty. An advertisement
in the *Leeds Mercury* in June 1728 says that:

A Gang of Good Packhorses, containing eighteen in number,
with their accoutrements and Business belonging to the
same, being one of the ancient gangs which has gone with
Goods from York, Leeds, and Wakefield to London, being
the Horses of Thomas Varley . . . etc.

are for sale. Such gangs could travel over the hills, not worried
by steep or rough ground and free on the moorland tops to
make diversions around patches of very bad ground. Packhorse
tracks thus tend to spread wide in a way which a walled road
cannot do. In many soft parts causeways of large flags or
stones were laid down and these are a frequent sight on our
hills. The tracks go up hill and down dale in a way entirely
foreign to tracks off the 'highland zone'.

The market road between Settle and Kirkby Malzeard, for
instance, starts at Settle, about 500 ft O D, and goes through
Arncliffe at 740 ft and Kettlewell at 750 ft, but between these
villages the way rises to 1,650 ft and 1,600 ft respectively.
Leaving Kettlewell, the traveller climbs to more than 1,750 ft
O D and, after a moorland crossing of 8 miles, he reaches a
stream at 750 ft, climbs to Middlesmoor at 950 ft, then down
to the River Nidd at 550 ft. The climbs over the fells to
Masham or Kirkby Malzeard reach 1,400 ft and 1,226 ft

respectively. This switchback route is in no way unique; most of the cross-dale market routes of which we are speaking rise to great heights on the uplands but generally manage to cross between 1,500 ft and 1,750 ft. Deep peat with uncrossable erosion gullies called haggs and a prolonged snow cover make almost any higher line than this impracticable.

With the improved performance of today's motor-cars in mind, a few of these ancient market ways have been made into motor roads; for instance, the old green track from Ramsgill in the head of Nidderdale across the moors to Masham is now a motor road, saving a great many miles and bringing Masham market within easy access of Nidderdale. At weekends the town-dweller enjoys the testing zigzag climbs to the tops and the stimulating run across the high moors, but we must hope and strive to keep most of these green ways for the generations who sooner or later are going to relearn the pleasure and benefit of walking on the quiet tops.[1]

In the days of the packhorses the journeys between some of the principal markets would take two or three days, and along these roads there are ancient inns or their ruins, often called the Packhorse Inn or the Packman, where abundant outbuildings allowed the unloading of the packs and many small closes could accommodate the ponies. The packman and his boy would sleep among the packs, but stories of theft are remarkably few and the whole trade seems to have been based upon honesty and trust (Illus. 21).

Within the broad pattern of market roads there is a complex of shorter tracks which link up most of the villages and which also breast the hills to reach outlying hamlets and farms. The market roads in many cases carry the name Jagger Lane or some variant of this, the 'jagger' being derived from the 'jaeger', hunter, as the sturdy German hunting ponies were used extensively for this work. There are, however, some green tracks named Badger Gate, Badger Stile and so on, and these remind us of a humbler traveller connected with the markets. The 'badger' was a small trader licensed to carry corn from the market to sell in small quantities to individual customers or in other markets. No doubt he would carry other goods as well as

corn, spices and smaller dry-salter's articles. He served those
for whom a market journey was more than their needs would
warrant.

The early development of the wool trade in centres like
Halifax and Kendal was based upon the 'brogger' or 'wool
driver' – the man with one or two packhorses who followed the
pattern of the 'badger', visiting farms and hamlets all over the
dales country, buying in small parcels of wool. These he took
to the clothiers in Halifax or Kendal market. The so-called
'Halifax Act' of 1552, restricting the dealing in wool to members
of the Staple, was soon changed, so that in 1555 exemption was
given for the wool driver and brogger; in fact they were then
established as an essential part of the industry. In a way they
are still represented by the wool buyer's motor lorry which
now makes its regulated visits to many of the remote farms
which have usable roads.

We have then a picture of our network of green roads carrying a regular traffic of gangs of packhorses going between
markets, feeding intermediate village markets and being known
all along the road. They carried news and gossip of a wider
world and were an important and welcome element in the dales
community. The broggers and badgers served the isolated
farms and hamlets in the same way, and in the later nineteenth
century their tradition was continued by the 'Scotsman' who
visited the same areas but carried his pack on his back and
traded mainly in haberdashery. A few of these men still have
their regular periodic rounds in the dales, but generally they
work with a small car which can get them over much of the
ground and can thus extend their area to an economic size.

We started this chapter with Torrington's comments on the
inn at Gearstones and its congregation of Scots drovers. This
was by no means an isolated picture. There are still many farms
on the fells which appear to be lonely beyond the reach of any
company, some, because of their isolation, having been
abandoned to fall into ruin. Yet some or these have in a past
age shared scenes as crowded and as lively as those at Gearstones. These were the inns along or near the great drove
roads, where drovers of Scottish cattle, farmers and butchers

met and the loneliness of the long 'drive' from Scotland was
relieved by the rare night of drink and song.

This droving trade, with its sturdy race of drovers, arose in
the late seventeenth century with the increasing demand for
meat in the English markets, particularly of the south. Young
cattle were collected from the Highlands, and in the eighteenth
century even from the Hebrides, and were gathered into the
great fairs or 'trysts' at a few centres such as Falkirk, Crieff and
Dumfries. Here the cattle were bought by English 'graziers'
in herds of many hundreds. The cattle were then driven quietly
to fairs in the north of England where farmers bought them for
over-wintering on their hill pastures, returning them next year
into the markets where they were bought by butchers or their
agents to be driven again to the meat markets of the Midlands
and around London.[2]

The drovers were men skilled in handling these wild cattle,
and a drover with a boy and two dogs would bring 40 or 50
beasts by quiet ways along the fells, avoiding villages and
cultivated ground, crossing rivers by fords, and caring for their
charges day and night. Usually a number of drovers would
combine to move with a herd of 100 or 200, making 10 to 12
miles a day and carrying food and the minimum of stores on a
pack pony. Most nights they slept out with the cattle, wrapped
only in their woollen plaids, but occasionally they had a livelier
night at some drovers' inn. Their staple food was oatmeal.

The drove roads are not as numerous as the market roads;
they run from north to south, crossing the borders into
England by the valleys of the Jed into the headwaters of the
Coquet, by Liddesdale to the source of the North Tyne, by
Eskdale and Annandale to the South Tyne and Eden, or from
Dumfries by Gretna or the fords across the Solway to Carlisle.
These were busy principal routes and the drove roads which
cross into the Yorkshire dales stem principally from the
Annandale and South Tyne way. The great road which came
from Bewcastle to Gilsland crossed the Irthing on to the
Pennines, going up the South Tyne valley into the headwaters
of the Tees. A broad green track is still preserved in part on
the west side of the river, crossing the big tributary of Maize

Beck near Birkdale, for long a house of call for the drovers. Farther down the dale, near Holwick, the tracks cross south-ward over the Lune and Balder, tributaries of the Tees, and near Grassholme the route divides. The westerly branch came by Sleightholme in the Greta valley, through upper Arken-garthdale and then between Melbecks and Reeth Moors into Swaledale. Over the moors to Askrigg in Wensleydale a road went by the Roman road to Gearstones, the road followed by Lord Torrington and already described. An alternative way was by the Stake and crossing upper Wharfedale and Litton-dale to Great Close on Malham Moor.

The easterly branch of the great drove road from Grassholme crossed Stainmore by Gilmonby, then over Barningham and Gayles moors and Richmond outmoor to Richmond. From Richmond forward roads took the cattle to the great fairs at Northallerton or Masham. There were routes on the west side of the Pennines which converged on Appleby and on Brough Hill near the head of the Eden valley, and thence to Malham, Settle or Lancaster.

The Great Close, which became the site of the drovers' fairs at Malham Moor, is a large enclosed pasture near Malham Tarn and to the east of it. It was part of the estates of Fountains Abbey, but after the Dissolution of the Monasteries it had come into the hands of the Lambert family. It was said to be the largest enclosed pasture in the country, being 'upwards of 732 acres in one Pasture, a great part of which is a fine rich soil, and remarkable for making Cattle both ex-peditiously and uncommonly fat'. At the opening of the seventeenth century it was used as an agistment, a pasture into which sheep, cattle and horses were taken from many farmers and grazed for a season. The stock using it were in fact 'boarded out' and looked after and fed by the owner of the agistment land.

A list survives from 1619 which gives us the 'Gyst taken into the great close of Malham more anno.dm. 1619'. This gives the name of every owner of stock and the number and kind of his animals, and over sixty people are named. The beasts are listed in groups by kind, as – 5 horses, with another 24 horses 'had

out of Lancashire', 5 'twinter [two year or two winter] Stagges',
8 'foles', 136 sheep, 58 made (full-grown) beasts, 73 twinter
beasts and 63 stirkes (bullocks), a total of 372 animals.[3] In the
eighteenth century the whole agistment was taken by a single
Skipton grazier, who used it as a gathering ground and market
for stock which he bought at the Scottish trysts. The Great
Close gatherings quickly took on the nature of a customary fair
or market to which other drovers, besides those employed by
Birtwhistle, brought their herds. The schoolmaster at Malham,
Thomas Hurtley, wrote in 1786 a book, *A Concise Account of
some Natural Curiosities in the Environs of Malham in Craven,
Yorkshire*, in which the text of 68 pages is followed by an
appendix of 199 pages on the life of General Lambert. However, in a footnote he says:

This Great Close, properly so called, was for many years
rented by Mr. Birtwhistle of Skipton, the celebrated Craven
Grazier, and on which you might frequently see 5000 head
of Scotch Cattle at one time. As soon as these were a little
freshened, notice was dispersed among the neighbouring
markets and villages, that a FAIR would be held in this
Field on a particular day; and lots being separated by guess
as nearly as could in such a manner be done to the wants and
wishes of any Purchaser, so much was fixed immediately
by the eye upon that lot, or so much per head, taking them
as they were accidentally intermixed upon an average. – To
a stranger this mode of bargaining will appear exceedingly
difficult and precarious; but it is amazing with what readiness
and exactitude persons accustomed to the business will
ascertain the value even of a very large Lot, frequently of
several hundreds together.

As soon as these were disposed of, a fresh Drove succeeded, and besides Sheep and Horses frequently in great
numbers, Mr. Birtwhistle has had Twenty Thousand head
of Cattle on this field in one summer; every Herd enticed
from their native soil and ushered into this fragrant Pasture,
by the Pipe of an Highland Orpheus.

If the Craven Graziers will yet esteem it a benefit to the

Country, Mr. Birtwhistle has the merit of being the first who traversed the Hebrides and the Isles and Counties in the North of Scotland and that at a hazardous period, in 1745, beginning a Commerce which by a gradual increase ever since, seems in some measure to have checked the ancient mode of breeding the LONG HORNED CRAVEN CATTLE, which were formerly held in the highest esteem.

Besides Mr. Birtwhistle who has had 10,000 head on the road from Scotland at one time, there are now several other Graziers who go to the Highlands on the same business, and vast quantities indeed are fed in every part of Craven for the markets in the populous Towns both in Yorkshire and Lancashire. To say the truth when fattened on these rich old Pastures, there is no Beef to equal them in fineness either of Grain or Flavour.

As the Great Close Fair flourished, a smaller related fair was established on Boss Moor, four miles to the south-east. Here the buyers of large parcels at Great Close often resold in small numbers to the local farmers who could feed just a few cattle on their upland pastures. It was this which gave the great stimulus to the improvement of the upland pasture by liming which has been noted in Chapter Five. On Great Close there was an alehouse for the drovers and farmers, now in ruins, and in like manner there was one on Boss Moor, which was called the Waste Inn. From both, roads radiate out in all directions, but the Great Close roads are long-distance droving roads, while those from Boss Moor lead mainly into the dales round about and to the markets at Skipton and Settle.

The droving trade and the occupation of grazier were flourishing through the eighteenth century and it is estimated that before the end of it somewhere around 100,000 cattle a year were moving into England. The nineteenth century saw a rapid decline brought about by a variety of factors. Commons were being enclosed, new roads were made, and some old drove roads were converted into the new hard road or even absorbed in a turnpike. Lengths of track across some of the moors were walled as enclosures were made on each side, and the loss of wayside grazing made the movement of the large herds of cattle impossible. The improvement of pasture over much of the country and the growth of stock-breeding also weakened the demand for Scottish cattle, and so the drovers ceased to come and a traditional occupation finished.

We can, however, in imagination take a wide and overall view of our Pennine uplands in the eighteenth century, and see a vast number of persons and animals traversing them by ways now almost unused except by the walker. The slow-moving herds with their attendant drovers, boys and dogs were at all times coming along the great north to south drove roads. East to west roads were mainly market roads, along which were moving the packhorse gangs; between the two, broggers and badgers, sturdy beggars, lime and peat getters and miners found their way among the hills. There must have been many meetings, long rests for news and gossip, friendly exchange and trust, or none of the trades could have survived. This picture of quietly-moving traffic over the lonely hills is a refreshing contrast to the crowded, noisy, smelly motor roads which are now penetrating more and more of the Pennine dales. For the present, however, we can walk many, many miles along these old high-level ways and think kindly upon those who made and used them in the past, resisting wherever we can the selfish requests which come from time to time for these ways to be 'modernized' so that the motorist, as well as the walker, can invade all the moorlands and fells.

CHAPTER NINE

An eighteenth-century estate manager

AT THE head of Airedale the village of Malham and the adjoining Malham Moor are today the most popular places of tourist attraction in the whole of the west Yorkshire dales. The village, of only 135 population (1961 census), has a cluster of grey stone houses on each side of Malham Beck, built around a village green, now unfortunately difficult to see at weekends beneath the rash of parked motor-cars and coaches. None the less it is an attractive village, with many good seventeenth-century buildings, narrow winding lanes among the houses and fields, and four bridges across the beck. Its history is long and well documented, as it was divided from the twelfth century into two manors east and west of the beck, Malham East being owned by the Augustinian canons of Bolton Priory and Malham West by the Cistercian monks of Fountains Abbey. It is now a village of farmers who breed dairy cattle and stock and run sheep on the upland pastures of Ewe Moor and Malham Moor.

Half a mile above the village Malham Beck appears, welling out of the foot of a limestone cliff 250 ft high and extending in a broad curved front to close the valley head. This cliff, called the Cove, overhangs and is one of the finest limestone features in Britain. A mile to the east of the village there is Gordale Scar, a keen rival to the Cove for the grandeur of its limestone scenery. These two features lie along the line of the Mid Craven Fault, a geological disruption which, through subsequent weathering, has provided a long succession of limestone cliffs and features running west to east across the Yorkshire dales (Illus. 22). On the north side of this fault are the Craven uplands, a vast plateau of limestone country above which rise the finer peaks of Ingleborough, Penygent and other of the dales mountains, and of which Malham Moor is a part.

The township of Malham Moor extends for about 11,000 acres and has no hamlet on it, but its population of 120 is scattered in isolated farms which originated in the tenth and eleventh centuries as Norse sheep farms. They continued as sheep farms of the Cistercian monastery of Fountains and after the Dissolution were continued, often in the family of the monastic tenants. The township of Malham Moor and much of Malham were bought by the Lamberts of Calton (the family of General Lambert of Civil War fame) and in 1697, after some intervening sales, was inherited by Lister of Gisburn. In 1785 what remained of the Fountains Abbey estates still in the hands of the Lamberts was sold to Lister, who thus became owner and lord of the manor of all Malham and Malham Moor (Fig 13).

The Listers were a very old west Yorkshire family, seated at Arnoldsbiggin near Gisburn until a removal, on inheritance, to the Low Hall at Gisburn. Thomas Lister (1685–1755) renamed this Gisburn Park, and with alterations and extensions it became the Lister home until its sale within the last ten years. Thomas Lister (1752–1826) was the Lister who completed the Malham estates and who replaced the old farm of Malwater-house, on the north bank of Malham Tarn, with a more formal and handsome house for use as a shooting box. This became the first stage in the architectural history of the present Tarn House which was only brought to its present form in 1862–85[3] (Illus. 23).

Thomas Lister, 1752–1826 (this form has to be used because for generation after generation the eldest son was called Thomas) was MP for Clitheroe, Lancashire, a family pocket borough, until 1790 when he retired to Gisburn Park and gave much of his time to the improvement of his estates. In 1794 he was High Sheriff of Yorkshire and in 1797, in recognition of his services in raising three troops of yeomanry, the 'West Riding Cavalry', he was created baron and took the title of Baron Ribblesdale of Gisburn Park, but was everywhere known as Lord Ribblesdale. It became his ambition to extend his estates

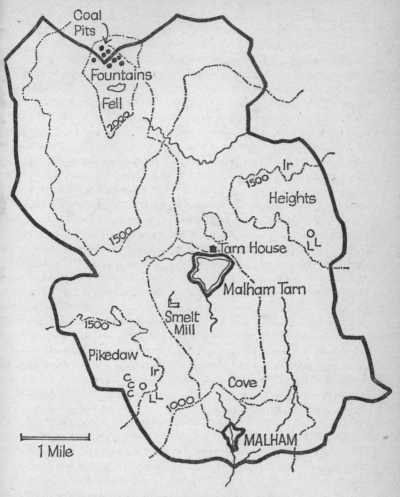

Fig 13. Malham and Malham Moor

Key:
O = calamine mines   C = copper mines
L = lead mines   Ir = iron mines

in such a way that he could ride from Gisburn Park to Malham Tarn over his own land, a distance of twelve miles in a direct line. Although he never achieved this, he did spend time, thought and money on his estate, and is said by Whitaker[2] to have planted 1,200,000 oak trees in and around Gisburn. He also planted extensively around Malham Tarn, but his agent reports in 1802 'except the Spruces the trees look sickly – larches are nearly all killed'.

Lister's Malham and Malham Moor estates covered between 11,000 and 12,000 acres, mostly above 1,200 ft OD and on the limestone plateau north of the Craven Fault but rising in Fountains Fell to 2,191 ft OD. His desire to develop these estates concurrently with Gisburn Park led to the appointment of an agent to live at Tarn House, collect rents and supervise a variety of activities. This agent was the Reverend Thomas Collins, DD, an eccentric. When Lister was at Brasenose College, Oxford, Collins was at Worcester College and though Collins (1748–1816) was four years older, the two became very close and affectionate friends. Collins was poor; his college in 1773 presented him to a small living at Compton Valance in Dorset, but he left the parish to a curate and only visited it twice in his life. Collins had probably accompanied Lister on the Grand Tour, as he says in one letter 'It is with infinite pleasure I red. your kind remembrance of me and our ancient Tours and Tournaments'. However it came about, Collins came to Gisburn Park, settled down to live there, and took part in the grandiose developments of the estate. There is more than a hint that he was regarded by the staff and some of the family as an interferer, and in 1784 the Townley family, close friends of Lister, presented him to the vicarage of Burnley, really to hold it until one of their own family was ready for it. This failed to get him away from Gisburn and he retained the Burnley living until his death, refusing in 1789 to give it up to one of the Townleys. He was a non-resident pluralist. In 1787 he had another brief appointment as Royal Chaplain in Ordinary to the Prince of Wales, later George IV, but this carried no pay. These various appointments may be evidence of Lister's growing influence rather than of Collins' merit, though in 1792 his old university gave him the degree of Doctor of Divinity.

Collins was called upon to oversee and largely to direct a variety of enterprises, and his long letters to Lister (later Lord Ribblesdale), which are always a mixture of news and reports of everything that is going on, present a man not perhaps specially skilled but certainly very willing, and through good commonsense able to manage such a complex of affairs as Ribblesdale put upon him. About 1802 Collins was sent from Gisburn Park to live at Malham Water House, soon to become Tarn House, to manage affairs on the Malham estates, though there is some suspicion that the move was made to get him away from Gisburn.[3]

The most homely side of his work was concerned with Tarn House and its staff during a time of considerable extension and re-planning. The Listers were becoming a wealthy family, with a rent roll of between £7,000 and £8,000 a year, though their solicitor says in 1796 that the mortgages and incumbrances on the property, due largely to Lister's extravagant schemes, amounted to nearly £80,000. The wages of idle and wasteful servants, indoor and out, at Gisburn Park amounted to £500 a year. Ribblesdale planned to replace the small Malham Water House with a large and more fashionable building on a re-strained Georgian plan. This new house had on the ground floor a large central room flanked at each side by a wing of two rooms' depth, thus giving in essence a five-room plan, three rooms on the front facing across the tarn to the south and two wing rooms to the rear. The front of the new house was completely symmetrical, with a three-sided bow window between balanced sash windows in the ends of the two wings. The building was in carefully-cut medium-grained sandstone with well-proportioned windows on ground and first floors. The entrance hall was in the rear portion of the east wing, and kitchens corresponded in the west wing. The roof space had attics for the servants and a service stairway was built in the mid-space of the west wing. The new building which Collins was called upon to oversee was not in such good stone as the first part of the house, some of it being fairly local, but the masoned stone for windows and doors was brought from a distance.

Collins was to enlarge the house, without disturbing its appearance, by filling in the space between the two wings, making a complete rectangular block and providing a butler's pantry, scullery and staff rooms. At the same time a rather imposing stable block, with rooms for stable and outdoor staff, was built some way above the house and called the High Stables.

In 1802 Collins was struggling with domestic difficulties both at Tarn House and at Gisburn Park and was at the same time very busy with the mines and with the estates in general. In one letter he says 'I want a resident Clerk. Many have offered for the Office but living at a distance will never do', and so he remained without assistance. He notes that he has not set foot out of the house for two days, being employed the whole time in writing letters about the estate. Later he is just as busy with guests. In June 1802 he was appointed a justice of the peace and some of his fellow justices, after his first Sessions, came to see him and to enjoy the shooting on his moors. His comments are usually caustic and critical. Of Mr Yorke he says:

I never remember him heartier – The Butter and Bread and Oatcake he devours at Breakfast is astonishing, and he eats most heartily of everything at dinner.

For Wilson of Eshton Hall he has bitter comment –

the Borough Ld. Hy. as Wilson is now universally denominated with Mr Preston (of Flasby) came to dinner. Wilson is more disliked than ever I saw a man in my life: indeed he provokes it by the most consummate Impudence and Vulgarity. We got some fine Trout and they were devoured to the fins and bones.

Some of the relations came and one, 'the Major' was 'in great spirits and by begging of me and of his own slaying graciously sent 8 Brace of fine Moorgame to be potted'. In that season Collins 'never remembered so many large and full-grown broods all over the Moors'. He records that he himself, not very good, got six brace out of eighty-five shots.

The butler, Binns, was a great worry to him, from his habits of drinking the best wine and entertaining his friends at the expense of Lord Ribblesdale.

> It is very inconvenient living in the same house with them. The extravagance and waste makes one shudder. Binns is the worst in encouraging it – they see more friends than you do at Gisburn Park and they are equally rude and noisy and disagreeable.

However,

> The great object of my disgust and uneasiness is removed – I believe if practicable to the Altar of Hymen. This secret was communicated to me this morning and I promised Silence, so pray indulge me. Most seriously do I wish to see a steady butler arrive.

The gardener at Gisburn was equally troublesome by

> letting everybody, workmen, haymakers, etc into the garden and not a currant, gooseberry, Raspberry have I seen, but one Tart all the year. Mother Binns made some currant jelly just in time.

Collins never really solved the problem of domestic service, and after the reign of the Binns family he had others as troublesome in other ways. There are occasional complaints which sound an unusual note, as when he breaks off in a business letter to say, 'Mrs Cooper has brought forth an Infant in the office – rather sooner than expected', and then continues with the business. He goes on to say 'the job between Chinese Gate and Poultry House Gate most substantially done; & Notices agst. Trespass put up'. This refers to Gisburn Park and presumably the birth was there and not at Tarn House.

Among all these worries the work on the Tarn House extensions was started and went well except that

workmen of all sorts are in the house but I really hope that Jno Robinson has completed his job famously. The men from Blackburn are repairing the damages to Ceilings by stretching the props which were indeed tremendously dangerous. Several of the Timbers had the Bark on and were rotten as tinder. They have put in new balks where a doubt remained so now all is secure.

Soon, however, writing about the High Stables, he has to report that

the slaters and workmen of all descriptions here is negligent and so ill provided. My spirits are nearly exhausted but I keep them all to it. Pray write, even in Wrath, but remember mercy.

The trouble was largely one of transport – it was very difficult, in bad weather almost impossible, to get materials to Tarn House – and not until Collins took over the getting of supplies did the work go on without long waits. For some years he had been keeping supplies in proper delivery at the mines and dealing with the transport of masses of calamine, so it was natural for him to mix in the builders' requirements with those of his orders for the mines. Thus we get, among mine accounts:

Jan 26 1807 to Jan 2 1808

1 quire of paper	1	4
6 paint pots	1	6
1 man & 1 horse leading stones all day	5	0
1 do 1 do to Gisburn	6	0
1 bottle turpentine from Skipton		4
Slates from Burndales	2	0
Nails from Skipton		2
Bigginstones from Skipton	10	0
2 men & 2 Carts leading stones & sand	10	0

2 do 2 do 1 day	10	0
1 cart load of sand from Lings	2	0
2 do do of Stone from Greet	8	0
Lats from Skipton	5	4
2 Tun of slate from Gargrave	14	0
1 man 1 horse 1 day	5	0
1 tun of slate from Skipton	12	6
3 tuns of slate from Gargrave	1 1	0
Tearing lats from Skipton	6	0
1 iron lock from Skipton		6
to sand to Malham Water House	6	0
5 days leading wood from Mr Lund to Malham	3 5	0
Wood from Malham to Malham Water House	10	0

There was trouble with the stables and also with the new kitchen.

The stable at Malham Water has been a fruitful subject of delay and God knows when it will be finished. The stable itself will consist of six small stalls and will I hope be coped tonight, the slaters having finished on Saturday last, but by a natural mistake in measuring, almost all the slate is gone without considering the ends. Two carts have gone today to Giggleswick for more slate and I hope by perseverance in this present work, the masons, the glaziers, the carpenters, the joiners and all grades will leave it fit for boarding and underdrawing in a fortnight.

To help matters, Collins fetched slate as mentioned and also, for the kitchen, fetched

Oven & Grates & other articles from Skipton	7	0
To sheet lead & Smook Jack from Malham to		
Malham Water House	3	0
To slate from warehouse at Gargrave	13	0
7 Load of lime from Maleson kill	3	6

To see them through the winter he also got in 723 loads of

coals from Gargrave to the house, this being house coal brought by canal from Leeds. When the workmen had finally left Collins turned to the job of painting, and there are long accounts for paints, mainly brown and black, but none for the labour of putting them on. The extensions and stables were in the end very satisfactory and rewarded all the effort they had demanded of the agent.

So far we have seen Collins acting as perhaps agents and secretaries all over the country were doing. In addition to these concerns, however, he was from 1802 called upon to direct mines of lead, zinc, iron and coal in conditions which really called for an experienced and competent mining engineer, and to take decisions on problems of transport and handling of materials in bulk which would have outfaced a smaller man.

On Malham Moor there are a few veins of copper and lead ores and two very unusual deposits of zinc and iron ores.[4] The copper veins had been worked in a crude way before 1698 and a lead mine called Richgrove was noted as at work in 1750. The copper veins were worked from a number of small shafts on the western part of the moor called Pikedaw, and in 1788 the miners at one of these came across a deposit of calamine, zinc carbonate. The miners had, in seeking copper, broken into a cavity in the limestone which they called the Great Gulph and from this had entered what soon proved to be a series of caverns. The calamine occurred on the floor of the caverns as a deposit of grey or white powder occasionally one or two feet thick. Its value for the brassmakers was recognized and in May 1792 Lister leased the mine for two years to some local men for the production of calamine. In 1795 the Cheadle Brass Company, who had been buying their calamine else-where, 'having been informed of the Calamine on Mr Lister's estate', asked for half a ton of the grey and white to be sent for a trial. The trials proved satisfactory and by June 1796 calamine was being sent regularly to Cheadle, but two difficulties had arisen – preparation of the ore and transport. The Cheadle Company required the ore to be calcined (roasted) before dispatch and, though many attempts were made, none was quite satisfactory.

The Leeds and Liverpool Canal, sanctioned by an Act of 1770, had been completed between Holm Bridge, Gargrave and Leeds by 1777 and connected with the Aire and Calder Navigation at Leeds, thus giving a through route to Hull and Gainsborough. A continuation of the canal as far as Burnley, Lancs, was in use before 1796, but the summit connexion completing it from Leeds to Liverpool was not made until 1816. Sending calamine to Cheadle was possible by two routes, one by Manchester as offered in a tradesman's card of May 1796 – to go to Gargrave, then canal to Burnley and carrier by road to Manchester. This was to cost from Gargrave to Manchester £1 11s 6d (£1.58) per ton. An alternative suggestion was Gargrave to Leeds by canal, Leeds to Gainsborough, and Gainsborough to Birmingham all by water transport; this came to £1 14s 4d (£1.72) per ton and was the route eventually chosen.

For two years calamine was sent this way to Cheadle; then, because of insufficient supplies and very inefficient calcining, the trade ceased and the miners turned from zinc to work in the Richgrove lead mine. It was four years before Collins in 1802 inherited this situation; he immediately made contact with Cheadle and was able to resume trade with them with an order for 400 tons of calamine. In explaining the situation to Lord Ribblesdale (as Lister now was), Collins points out that as the mines are on wild and high moorland (about 1,600 ft OD) the calamine was both wet and dirty and as a result the sacks in which it was sent away rotted and were good for only one journey. Eventually he bought and used treacle casks. They must therefore build a drying kiln and could combine with this a proper calcining furnace. He was then faced with correspondence, interviews, demonstrations and technical advice which, with no one knows what patient study, he mastered. He then started the conversion of a large house in Malham village into 'Calamine House', equipped with furnaces for drying and calcining and all else necessary.

The output of the mine could not be increased because of the extreme difficulty of access by a narrow creepway from an old copper shaft – 'the Mens' Roads into the chasm are most extremely dangerous as well as difficult'. Seen now from the inner end, they certainly tax the skill of a good caver. There were three principal caverns, named, by their length in yards, Chasm 104, 44 and 84, all communicating and with several side passages as well. It was Collins' idea to have all this surveyed and then to choose a spot on the surface from which to sink a commodious shaft into one of the caverns. The surveying was not at first successful. One of his men, Dawson, 'set off with the new invented Dial and his Spirit Level with Compasses etc, and lo! he durst not go down'. A miner was brought from Arkengarthdale lead mines after two others, including the schoolmaster, had made 'surveys', and found many errors in these, but 'these men are as near as possible in every line and direction'. However, the new shaft was sunk in 1806 and proved to meet Chasm 44 exactly in the centre at a depth of over 70 ft. From then on production was easier, and Collins' main difficulties turned to the calcining furnaces.

As early as 1795 Lister had tried to make white paint from the best of the white calamine, which

> for the sake of humanity I trust will be found a complete substitute for that baneful article, white lead . . . It answered well for house painting externally, and the whiteness improves by time . . .

The paint trade, which grew fairly quickly, stimulated a search for ochre as a pigment, and remarkable deposits were found not far from the calamine mine as well as at other places on the estate. Collins had the job of opening up and managing all these, but with too little technical knowledge the paints produced failed against competition, although Ribblesdale was given the Royal Society of Arts silver medal in 1808. Collins found other outlets for the ochre of several qualities and the mines, both calamine and ochre, continued until 1830. The caverns in Pikedaw by that time were exhausted and the ochre deposits were nearly done, at least of all the better quality. It was reported that more than 2,000 tons of calamine were sold to the brassmakers before 1808 and nearly as much was sold in later years.

One minor sideline illustrates the alertness of Collins, not only in large but also in smaller matters. Search was made for any other mines of calamine within the Ribblesdale estates and one or two minor occurrences were found on parts of Malham Moor. In one of these the calamine was in solid crystalline form, mainly stalagmitic on the floor of a cavity in a vein, but some occurred as stalactites, called by Collins 'watricles' on the parallel of icicles. These included a few which were coloured green or blue by the presence of copper salts, the vein being a slender one of copper ores. Collins had these watricles very carefully collected and sent them to a Bond Street lapidary who reported that they could be cut and polished. Collins found sufficient to supply the sequins for a unique court dress for Lady Ribblesdale. Other examples sent from time to time to be cut were made into a variety of dress ornaments. The supply, however, was always scanty. We are not even sure today just where the coloured calamine was obtained, and many amateur mineral collectors have sought it in vain.

As the business of the mine became more complex and the local men less competent to deal with the new demands, Collins sought help and brought in miners, a few from Arkengarthdale in north Yorkshire and one or two, particularly 'diallers' (surveyors), from the Burnley coalfield. Some of the incomers adapted themselves to the new conditions and helped to make the mines a partial success, but others with experience only in the coal mines became somewhat of a burden. However, with the increased demand for coal at Calamine House and the cost of coal and its transport from the canal at Gargrave, there was good reason to look for fresh and cheaper sources. The coals of Fountains Fell were soon discovered and the coal miners were in a position to develop them on sound lines. By 1807 a good colliery was opened out from a number of small shafts and supplies sufficient for local use were obtained. The work was at first in the hands of Watson, a man brought from Worsley, of whom the agent to the Marquis of Stafford had said 'he is a laborious, sober, honest man'. He was already in charge of the zinc mine, and the two responsibilities proved too much for him and he soon returned to Worsley. In fact, the agent had warned that he had no experience of superintending more than four or five men, and Collins had taken a great risk in employing him – one of his poorer judgements. Another foreman was got for each concern and the colliery soon became very active with production round about 10,000 loads a year.

The coal was from two seams of mixed quality, much of the poorest being sold for lime burning (see Chapter five), some of the better round the local dales for house coal and some being taken for the calcining house. When Collins learned that zinc smelters and brassmakers used coke, he had a rather unique 'coke oven' erected near the pits on Fountains Fell and tried to make coke there for Calamine House. Although the place shows signs of a fair amount of use, his experiments with coke were not in the end successful and he returned to the use of raw coal. This colliery is at 2,000 ft OD, so the difficulties of weather which Collins had to face can be imagined.

Still another idea of his led him into more commitments. During all this time on the Moor a number of small lead mines, mainly Richgroves at Pikedaw and mines on Middle House Heights, were working, and although there were the ruins of an old smelt mill not far from the Tarn the lead ores were sent away to be smelted. Most was taken to a small mill at Kilnsey where small parcels could be dealt with speedily; some was carried to Kettlewell, but occasional parcels were sent to the Duke of Devonshire's mill at Grassington Moor, where the smelting was by reverberatory furnace, the others smelting by ore hearth. The smelted lead was generally taken to Pateley Bridge or to Skipton for sale. Collins saw the advantage of having his own smelt mill at Malham, so the old mill was rebuilt, this time with a short flue up the hillside and a fine but stumpy chimney on the hill crest. This is still standing and is both a landmark and a fine industrial monument (Illus. 25). The mill unfortunately has been destroyed and is now only a heap of rubble.

The lead accounts follow the local pattern of the district, with no unusual item.

Sept. 15 1806. To repairing the shaft		5	0
To getting nineteen pieces and two stone of lead at eighteen Pounds per ton	17	4	7
To Driving a drift three fathom at ten shillings a fathom	1	10	0
To Joseph Boothman to 54 Days at 3/6 p Day	9	9	0
To Milles Knowles to 55 days at 3/– p Day	8	5	0
To William Silverwood to getting lead	17	14	5
To smelters wages Richard Weary 14 days at 3/–		2	2	0
To John Beecroft to 14 days at 3/– p day		2	2	0

And so they continue, with odd sums for baskets, carriage, timber and other normal items. The scale of the mining was never large, but it seemed to suffer less interruptions and difficulties than the other ventures, probably because this was primarily a lead-mining area and skilled miners were available for any work there might be.

Collins was able to engage better managers for the mines, both zinc and coal, and his later letters show him becoming more absorbed in Ribblesdale's finances and more inclined to accept the reports of his managers on the mines and other concerns. He also became much more critical of the time Ribblesdale was spending away from his estates, and particularly of his new preoccupation with a yacht. Lord Ribblesdale in 1812 was on the South Coast, at his house at Stoke Cliff, near Dartmouth, suggesting many schemes for a cruise, and Collins replies to him with the candour that only an older man and a very close friend could use. Ribblesdale must have sent him an outspoken letter, for Collins replies to him in these terms:

My dearest L,

If the most affectionate anxiety for your safety, interests, welfare and happiness be evidence of ill humour and checks to a cordial communication I must plead guilty and submit myself to the mercy of my Judge.

He then comments on the return from the south and says it might be done by sailing from Dartmouth to Scarborough, or,

preferring Lancashire as I do, from Dartmouth to Liverpool and from Liverpool to the Orkneys for fresh air I can only object personally to be of the Party.

My opinion is the Income is adequate to almost any moderate expense with a determined economy and if you are resolved to devote a part of it among the Navigators and will neglect the dearest interest of the Family – Be it so. You never will receive from me anything more than an earnest wish that Money was otherwise bestowed. I am all impatience to learn your destination and intentions.

A new butler has arrived at G.P. and I will endeavour to give him a clue to the evil and to impress upon his heart the determination of yr Ldship and Lady R. to overturn the disgraceful and wasting Profligacy of the family Customs.

Adieu – With begging the sincerest effusions of a friendly Heart to Lady R. and the dear children and yrself believe me to be as assuredly I am, my dear L. Your ever faithful and affect: T.C.

This is the last letter we have from him, and the only other note is a rent roll which appears to be in his handwriting. His letters show his complete devotion to the estate and to Lord Ribblesdale. A characteristic letter wanders from subject to subject in no particular order – the rents, mines, fishing and shooting, builders, matters on the magistrates' bench, personalities, and inquiries about the children and family and so on. His was a mind teeming with a vast complex of business and often feeling the weight of too much responsibility, but through it all he managed to establish industries and to exploit the resources of a large estate in a remarkable way. It would be good if we could have known much more of the personal life of this remarkable man.

CHAPTER TEN

Three country schools

THE YORKSHIRE dales are fortunate in the number of small
endowed schools which they have had from the sixteenth
and seventeenth centuries. A few have arisen from chantry
schools, the endowments of which were saved at the sup-
pression of the chantries and transferred to small local schools.
Some were endowed by dalesfolk as 'grammar' schools and a
few were founded by a local yeoman or merchant for the
education of the children of his village. Several of these
schools survive, either as public or grammar schools like
Sedbergh, Giggleswick, or Ermysted's Grammar School,
Skipton, or as primary schools. The histories of three of the
smaller schools will illustrate something of the variety of
origin one finds among them.

Two events during the sixteenth century had great significance for life in the dales area, the Pilgrimage of Grace in
1536 and the Rising of the North in 1569. Both these risings
were limited to northern areas, both failed, and in both the
punishment of participants was severe though selective. The
Pilgrimage of Grace was in essence a revolt of peasants ap-
parently started by and connected with the ejection of monks
from the smaller abbeys, but actually it was the culmination of
a generation of growing discontent and fear. The attempts of
lords of the manor and landed gentry to enclose commons
had been met by riots in which the peasants had destroyed
fences and re-used the enclosures. Of the rioters in Airton in
Airedale 'the most partie were women and children', and
eighty were apprehended for three separate riots. This, in
1534, was only one instance of widespread trouble, and a
commission appointed by the King reported that from the

area of upper Airedale there were imprisoned, for similar riot, forty freeholders of Lord Cumberland in Skipton Castle, twenty tenants of Lambert in Sandall Castle and fourteen tenants of the Abbot of Furness in Wressle Castle. All these were from a small area around Airton and Winterburn in Airedale. Rumours circulated by the smaller gentry, who held positions or benefits under the monasteries, took advantage of these discontents and led the people to believe that their parish churches were threatened and that taxes would be imposed on the services of baptism, marriage and burial, as well as on cattle and in other ways.

The great rising of October 1536, stimulated by Aske of York, was centred upon Wensleydale, with other gatherings and assemblies in Dentdale and around Kendal, in upper Wharfedale and in most parts of the western dales. Two armies marched on October 16th, on the east and west of the Pennines. York and Pontefract were captured on the east, and on the west the Dentdale men and their associates faced Lord Derby at Preston. Between these two armies a large contingent led by Jaques and Fawcett of Kettlewell and Littondale had crossed Wharfedale and Littondale, and by marches along old green roads had arrived at Salley and Whalley abbeys where they had put back the displaced monks.

This rising was dispersed by the promise of reform of the feared abuses and a general pardon for the rioters, but discontent and the failure to implement the promises caused a slight resurgence in January 1537, particularly in Wharfedale and Airedale where assemblies were called by notices nailed to the church doors at Burnsall, Linton, Rilston and Gargrave. About 200 people responded to the summons but were dispersed by the Earl of Cumberland with his followers from Skipton. Some of the rioters were imprisoned at Skipton and this, with the execution of the prior and abbot of Salley and some of the smaller gentry like Hammerton and Tempest, with some leaders, Lord Dacre and others, ended the matter.

The second event was more political, an attempt by some of the northern nobles to secure the succession of Mary Queen of Scots to the English throne. The principal leaders of this rebellion were the Duke of Norfolk and the Earls of North-umberland and Westmorland. Northumberland and Norfolk were executed and Westmorland went into exile; about 800 of the ordinary folk were executed near their own villages as an example of the cost of rebellion. There were hangings at Rilston, Hanlith, Linton and Threshfield in the part of the dales we are discussing and 231 in the neighbouring Rich-mondshire. The estates of Northumberland and Westmorland, which included much of the dales, were confiscated to the Crown along with those of the Nortons of Rilston and some others. These various estates were later granted to the Cliffords of Skipton or sold to tenants who became freeholders. In some cases a whole manor was thus sold and the freeholders became the lords of the manor (see Chapter Three). It was these new freeholders who in the late Elizabethan and early Stuart years prospered well; some of them endowed our country schools.

The family of Fawcett, one of whom led the local army of the Pilgrimage of Grace, was an old one in Littondale. The name occurs in Fountains Abbey accounts in the fifteenth century and also in the list of Clifford tenants who went to Flodden Field in 1513. Fawcetts had been tenants of Upper Hesleden on Penygent side at least as early as 1456. In the court rolls of Litton, which include the township of Halton Gill, Richard Fawcett is one of the tenants in 1534. In the seventeenth century the family owned land in Halton Gill and had bought Upper Hesleden after the Dissolution of the Monasteries. The family of Fawcett remained in Halton Gill for several generations, but as in so many of the dales families a son was frequently sent out into the world to find a living in trade. In the latter part of the sixteenth century the two brothers, Henry and William Fawcett, left the dales to enter into trade in Norwich. Here they made a good living and Henry in time became an alderman of the town. In his will of 1619 he remembered the place of his birth and left an annuity of £10 a year to the clergyman of Halton Gill Chapel. This was a chapel-of-ease of Arncliffe Church, certainly an ancient foundation although the first documentary reference to it is only in 1577. The will stipulated that the £10 was for a minister of Halton Gill for reading the services and for teaching poor men's children. It was provided by a rent charge upon an estate at Roughton in Norfolk, and it is still paid from there.[1]

This annuity might have accomplished very little if William had not, by his will of April 27th, 1630, added considerably to it. In the will he mentions a debt of £630 owing to him by his nephew Marmaduke Fawcett, secured on a long lease of the farm of Over or Upper Hesleden, which should be discharged if Marmaduke, within two years, made arrangements and assurance for an annual payment of £18 6s. 8d. (£18.33).[2] Of this sum, £13 6s 8d (£13.33) a year was to be paid to a Master of Arts or other well-qualified scholar who should preach in Halton Gill Chapel and catechize the younger sort of people on Sunday in the chapel. He was also to teach the rudiments of grammar and learning to the children of the parish on weekdays. The remaining £5 was divided, £4 to the poor of Littondale and £1 for two sermons on the morning and afternoon of November 5th, one at Arncliffe Church and one at Halton Gill Chapel.

For the weekday teaching William had already built a small building abutting on the west end of Halton Gill Chapel, in which the master should live and teach. Over the door it has a tablet which carries the date 1626 and the initials W.F. A 'terrier' of the school and chapel property in 1781[3] describes the school as:

The Curate's house which is also the schoolroom adjoining the west end of the chapel, the length of the front side 17 Feet and the length of the west side 18 Feet 2 Inches within the walls, built of Grit Stone and covered with Slates. The Wood of the Roof a great measure of oak. It contains four rooms viz. two low rooms (ground floor) and two high rooms. The two low rooms are parted by a Gritstone wall and the two high rooms by a Lath and Plaster Partition and laid with Boards the whole, having seven windows and opening for another when required. (Illus. 27.)

William Fawcett in his will expressed the wish that, if a

Master of Arts could not be obtained for the school, then some other 'able and well qualified person' should be found and preference should be given to a member of his own family if a suitable one could be found. The accommodation was somewhat cramped but the sum of £23 6s 8d (£23.33) a year in 1630 was good pay. The original endowment was charged on Upper Hesleden Farm, and very soon the farm became in fact the curate's glebe, but as his duties at the school kept him in the village every day the farm was let to a tenant at an improved rent which in 1826 was £24 and by 1894 had become £45.

Until 1847 the curate lived in the house and taught the children in one schoolroom, the numbers being about ten or twelve. After 1847, however, a master was appointed to the school on the original salary of £10 a year and the curate was transferred to Arncliffe and served the Halton Gill Chapel from there. In this very remote and tiny school there was room for the eccentric and unusual master – only serious devotion would keep a curate and schoolmaster in this position for a long period, in one case for seventy years of service.

We have no complete record of the early schoolmasters, but from the parish registers and other documents we glean a few names. In 1673 John Hargreaves, minister of Halton Gill, was buried; in 1690 Francis Bryer, in 1711 Mr Tomson, in 1714 Humphrey Dickinson and in 1722 John Hogget are mentioned as being at those dates curate of Halton Gill and master of the school. In 1737 the first of the eccentrics was appointed as curate and master, one Miles Wilson, who in August in the same year married Dorothy Lambert, a farmer's daughter of Halton Gill. Wilson served the curacy and school for forty years and brought up two sons who entered the Church. The eldest son, Edward, went to Christ's College, Cambridge, and after a good career as a student was appointed tutor to the two sons of the Earl of Chatham with whom he remained for eight years. In 1773 he accompanied the younger son, William Pitt, to Cambridge and resided with him there. Pitt later secured for Wilson canonries at Windsor and

Gloucester, with a rectory at Binfield, all good preferments. The younger son, Thomas, after Cambridge became a pluralist with the livings of Saham, Whaddon and Godney, all described as 'rich'.[4]

It is seen from a surviving list of Wilson's books that he was a man of scholarly inclinations, as they included several in Hebrew, Latin and Greek. Although he was not an MA it is clear that he came well within William Fawcett's requirements of an 'able and well qualified person'. Miles Wilson's most curious achievement was his little book *The Man in the Moon*. This described an imaginary journey of a Halton Gill cobbler, Israel Jobson, who went to the summit of the neighbouring Penygent. From it a ladder enabled him to climb through space on to the surface of the moon. He was able, after exploring the moon, to use it as the starting-point for a long journey through the solar system. Although the story verges on the ridiculous and fantastic, the book includes good descriptions of the solar system as understood at that time and might well have been used in his school. Copies are now almost unknown because Wilson at one time called in and destroyed every copy he could trace. Other of his eccentricities took the form of contriving mechanical toys and models and of fine wood carvings. These would both appear strange in the curate of such a remote area. His 'weather glass' caused much wonder and his neighbours greatly admired the carving in wood of an ape blowing a trumpet. Other mechanical wonders credited to him owe more to vivid rustic marvel than to actual fact.

Wilson was followed by an equally unusual man, Thomas Lindley, born at Hipperholme, near Halifax. He was not a university man but was ordained by Archbishop Markham of York who described him as a 'literate person', and certainly his few books included works in Hebrew and Greek. He lived unmarried for seventy years in the tiny schoolhouse. His meagre income was supplemented by small local interests, keeping the parish accounts (these are in a beautiful copperplate script), taking a few older youths for training in reading and accounts, and helping parishioners with written work such as cataloguing and valuing their goods for a sale, keeping the records of a sale and so on.

During Lindley's time, in 1781, a terrier of all the school and chapel property was needed and Lindley produced a survey beautifully written and meticulously accurate. His school is measured, as already quoted, to the inch and the same was done for the school farm (Over Hesleden); its buildings and outbuildings were as accurately measured. The materials of buildings, walls and floors are noted and the nature of fields and enclosures. During his tenancy of the school there was a growing desire in Halton Gill that girls should be allowed to have the privilege of attending, so Lindley put a case to the vicar of Arncliffe and he took a legal opinion.[5] In 1791 it was decided that the endowment was 'no bequest for a petty school nor for writing and arithmetic'. The requisition that the master should be versed in Latin and Greek is a higher description than a teacher of English and Accounts. The word

Learning ... implies the learned languages Latin and Greek and all such knowledge as is connected therewith particularly Geography and Chronology ... The Female children of a Parish cannot be the objects of a Grammar School.

Finally, if the master had not enough pupils to engage his whole time, he could teach writing and arithmetic for a small fee, to both boys and girls. On this basis girls were admitted to the school and a small weekly fee was charged.

When Lindley was appointed curate there was no one in charge of Hubberholme Chapel in Langstrothdale, and it became customary to serve this from Halton Gill, Lindley riding or walking over the fells every week when possible after an early service at Halton Gill. At his death in 1847 a curate was appointed and the schoolmaster was made a separate appointment at the original £10, the remainder going to the curate.

In the nineteenth century the population of Littondale declined. At the 1811 census, Halton Gill had a population of

141, but this dropped to 88 by 1831, to 74 in 1901; it remained around 80 or just under through the nineteenth century and was still 76 in 1951. The closing of some upland farms and movement of population brought it down to only 37 in 1961. Its neighbour, Litton, has dropped from 114 in 1851 to 59 in 1951 and 53 in 1961. The number of scholars dropped in the same way, between a maximum of about 19 down to 4 or 5. Little is known of the progress of the school after 1847 until after the Education Acts, when the schoolmaster was required to keep a log book and the school was visited by HM inspectors.[6] An inspector in 1884 reported that children of ten years were only doing work that would be appropriate to those of eight years, but a close examination of the log book suggests that this could be largely due to the time lost because of the weather and rigorous climate. Halton Gill is 1,000 ft above sea level and is surrounded by fells which rise to 2,231 ft OD and 2,048 ft OD on the west and south and to 1,959 ft OD and 1,985 ft OD on the north and east (Illus. 1). The average rainfall may exceed 60 ins in a year and the snow cover is long. Children coming from remote farms, some of which are at 1,400 ft OD, missed a lot of attendances because it was impossible to get to school, the tracks being interrupted by snowdrifts or flooded streams. In 1885 there were a total of $12\frac{1}{2}$ weeks when children were prevented from reaching school; in 1886, including the absence of boys at lambing time and hay time, May and August, there were $14\frac{1}{2}$ weeks, and in 1888, which was a bad year, 21 weeks were lost when attendance fell from between 14 and 16 to between 5 and 9.

About 1877 a school was built lower down the valley at Arncliffe which soon had about 40 pupils but only 1 master, 2 monitors (aged 13) and a sewing mistress. At Litton also a small school was opened in 1883 and this had more effect on the Halton Gill School attendance. In 1891 a mistress was first appointed at Halton Gill who introduced geography and replaced grammar by object lessons in domestic economy. However, she only stayed 15 months and her successors only 3 months, 12 months and 2 months in turn, then 2 years and 5 months passed before a more settled teacher was found. The school became a primary for the intermediate area in 1902 and continued its very quiet service until 1958, when it finally closed, leaving Arncliffe as the only school for Littondale, Litton having closed in 1928.

The second school at which we shall look is at Kettlewell, a village near the head of Wharfedale. The school is one which has been in essence a township school. As we saw in Chapter Three, Kettlewell manor in the latter part of the sixteenth and early seventeenth centuries had been held by the Crown until 1656 when it was transferred to and held by the Trust Lords on behalf of the freeholders. While still administered by the Crown the working of lead mines within the manor had been granted to Humphrey Wharton along with many mines in Swaledale. Wharton was closely associated with Sir Solomon Swale of Grinton who worked some of the Swaledale mines until the Civil War. However it came about, Sir Solomon became interested in the Kettlewell mines and eventually his cousin Philip Swale, agent to Lord Wharton, succeeded to the lease of the Kettlewell area. Philip brought into a new lease Francis Smithson, like himself a Quaker, and then in a new partnership Anthony Barker, a miner from Derbyshire. The families of Swale, Smithson and Barker kept their connexion with Kettlewell for several generations.

Solomon Swale was the Member of Parliament for Aldborough who proposed the motion calling for the restoration of Charles II, and it was on this occasion that he received his title. It may have been in commemoration of this event that he gave a school to Kettlewell. Whatever the date, and it is not known precisely, Solomon Swale built a schoolhouse at his own expense on the waste of the manor for teaching the children of the village. He gave five sheep gates on Middlesmoor, one of the township's common pastures, the income to be used for the repair of the schoolhouse. Philip Swale left by will, in 1687, £5 to the school and £10 for training apprentices. Small parcels of land were added to the endowments until by 1720 they amounted to 28 acres.[7]

In the enclosure award of 1802 the school received for its five sheep gates an allotment of just over $4\frac{1}{2}$ acres of land and a half sheep gate on each of the two pastures Whernside and Top Mere. The land was let for £4 or £5 yearly. At some time 8 acres of land had been given, with a rent charge upon it for paying the master to teach three poor children in the school. There is no record of the progress of the school beyond the occasional name of a master, but by the end of the eighteenth century the interest of the inhabitants was waning, leaving the vicar to carry the whole management of the school and to appoint the masters. There were then about forty scholars and by 1860 the need for a better-qualified master was beginning to be felt. The vicar formed a committee of parishioners to raise money for an increased salary for such a master. Kettlewell was experiencing a period of relative prosperity in its mines and there had been an influx of miners, with their strong leanings to Nonconformity, so that the majority of the vicar's committee were found to be Wesleyan Methodists. They disagreed strongly with the vicar's plans for the school rules and for a Sunday school, and especially his demand that the master should be a member of the Church of England. This disagreement developed into a minor feud, and the committee took the school and its management into its own hands and collected the income. Their first problem was the state of the building, now in a very bad condition and far too small, the school now having more than fifty pupils. The vicar persuaded the Charity Commissioners to appoint himself and his church-wardens as trustees of the school; then they proceeded to buy a piece of land from the Trust Lords on which they proposed to build a new school to be a national (C of E) school. To avoid the obligations of the Endowed Schools Act the new building was near, but not on, the site of the old school; a fund had been collected in the village for the new school. The old school, because of its condition, was condemned and was pulled down, but the villagers resisted the new school with sufficient force to secure that it was pulled down also, before completion.

With help from the National School Society the vicar now built a new school on the site of the old one and declared it to be a national school. This was in 1876, but the Charity Commissioners stepped in to rule that a building on the old site could not be anything but a free school and the villagers so resented the master, mistress and managers being restricted to Church members that they withdrew their children and the new school closed after barely two months of use. The building, in typical Victorian Gothic, remained unused except for a weekly bank and an occasional concert, until recently when it was converted to a hostel type guest house for young folk.

In the autumn of 1876 the Education Department ruled that Kettlewell must appoint a schoolmaster or a school board would be formed. The vicar would not yield, so the townspeople appointed a young Nonconformist whom they liked and re-opened the school in a hired room. In 1883 a school board was formed and a school built just out of the town which is still active as the county primary school for all the upper dale.

The master appointed was Carradice, who started a re-markable career which lasted all his life (February 4th, 1884, to September 1923), during which time he became an important influence in the village and also tried many experiments in practical education. Like the school at Halton Gill, the Kettle-well school was to a large extent at the mercy of the weather. Floods on the roads and snow on the hills kept children away, but a very regular deterrent was the lateness of the haymaking. The summer holiday was theoretically calculated to allow both boys and girls to give help in this most vital harvest, but in twenty-one of his thirty-nine years Carradice noted in his log book that the hay crop was 'backward' and holidays extended.[8]

The school board was elected from the villagers; it was poor and unable to provide much more than the very minimum. The school started with one blackboard as its total equipment and there was a long struggle before this could be increased. The first help Carradice had was from a young girl, aged twelve, who became a monitor, attending before and after school hours for her own lessons. This was three years after the opening of the school. In 1896 she finished her apprenticeship and became a Queen's Scholar and so went to a training college. The inspectors more than once threatened that unless an assistant were appointed the school must close. In 1902 he got an unqualified woman to teach the infants.

Carradice was quick to use the environment of the school and the creatures and plants of the area in his lessons. From the gamekeeper he got an otter, a golden eagle and a brown owl; moles, voles, rabbits, spiders, trout, all were brought to school and studied and their natural haunts were visited. He instilled in his pupils, along with sound formal lessons, a love of nature and a sense of moral values which stayed with them all their lives. Carradice gave this, the only board school in the dale, a great reputation which his successors have worked hard and with success to continue.

Unlike Halton Gill and Kettlewell schools, Threshfield School was founded by a man of whose life there is good knowledge and documentation. Matthew Hewitt, rector of Linton, was a son of William Hewitt of Threshfield, a member of a yeoman family that had been well established in the township for many previous generations and long remained important. William Hewitt had inherited land in Threshfield which had formerly belonged to the Cliffords, for when Francis Lord Clifford sold the Threshfield estates in 1608 the two families of Hewitt and Hammond were the principal purchasers. Matthew Hewitt had been of sufficient consequence to become one of the trustees to whom the Crown sold the manor of Kettlewell for resale to the freeholders, and his name figures in other connexions as a man of substance. His will, made on April 26th, 1674, recites that he has lands, tenements, etc, in Linton, Threshfield, Kettlewell and Starbotton in Wharfedale, and also lands and coal mines which came to him from his wife, in Great Gomersall, Burstall, Darton and Clementhorpe in the West Riding. All these were left to his daughter Mary for her life, then to her heirs, but in default of heirs the lands and property in Gomersall and Birstall went to his nephew, Richard Hewitt of York, attorney, son of his brother Richard, who had been an alderman of York. The estates were charged with the provision of £12 10s (£12.50) a year to each of four scholars of St John's College, Cambridge, to be chosen from 'my nearest kindred' first, secondly from boys of his name, and thirdly to be elected by his nephew Richard and his heirs and the master and fellows of St John's College. The first choice was always to be made from Threshfield School, which he established by the next clause in his will. A yearly sum of £30 was to be put to the building of a schoolhouse near the gate of his field, Gaine Bank, which is near the river towards the Linton boundary. This was to be a free school, with £20 a year for a master and £10 a year for an usher. The schoolhouse was to be enclosed in a garden surrounded by a stone wall which Richard's heirs had to maintain, along with the schoolhouse, for ever. The master and usher were to be nominated by members of the Hewitt family, or failing them, by the Archbishop of York.

The school was built and is a handsome building with fine mullioned windows and an attractive porch with an upper room in which the schoolmaster lived (Illus. 27). It was regarded as a grammar school, free to all boys who applied for teaching in Latin and English grammar, but for writing and accounts they had to pay. Until 1730 boys were sent yearly to St John's College but they then became fewer and between 1790 and 1820 only three exhibitions were awarded. Because of the lack of scholars the Cambridge University Commissioners were allowed in 1859 to abrogate the special terms of the will and the endowment went to the general revenues of the college. The school produced a few boys who found big preferment – Dr William Craven became Master of St John's College, Dr Dodgson Bishop of Elgin, and William Sheepshanks a prebend of Carlisle and Lincoln.

The management of the school and the obligations to repair it and to pay the usher were not always strictly observed by the Hewitt descendants, and in 1799 the churchwardens, constables and several freeholders of Threshfield, Linton and Grassington agreed to start legal proceedings against David Swale and James Hartley, the then representatives of the Hewitt bequests, for refusing to repair the school and pay the master's and usher's salaries. On August 16th, 1800, a larger group of inhabitants issued a notice demanding that the repairs not done, the salary of the usher John Wildman, unpaid since 1794, and the value of trees cut and taken from the garden of the school, be paid before October 1st or the matter would be remitted to the Attorney-General for him to compel the performance of the trusts. John Wildman had been licensed by the Archbishop of York to be usher, and he was associated with the complaint to represent his own and the master's case. The matter was placed before Henry Wigglesworth, clerk, as arbitrator with a bond in £200 to accept his decision. This, given August 28th, 1801, was that David Swale should pay before October 1st to John Wildman £70 of arrears of salary and his costs of £15, and Wildman should pay £1 11s 6d (£1.57), the costs of the arbitration.

There was a little further bother about the nomination of an usher to follow Wildman, the surviving Hewitt, Henry, of Paythorne, after two years suggesting a name not acceptable to the villagers, but Hewitt agreed at last to nominate Richard Sheepshanks of Linton, a man already for two years acting as usher at the school and well liked by all the parents. This was accepted and the discontent ceased. By 1865 an inquiry revealed that no instruction was being given except in elementary subjects, that reading was taught free but for writing 4½d (2p) a week was paid. It continued now as an elementary school and by a scheme under the Charitable Trusts Acts the school, under the name of the Threshfield School Foundation, was placed in the charge of five governors, appointed locally, and was to be administered as a public elementary school under the Elementary Education Act of 1870. The religious instruction was to be given 'according to the principles of the Christian faith' and the school was vested in the Charity Commissioners, not the Ecclesiastical Commissioners, and so was definitely not a Church school as was claimed by some people at the beginning of this century.[9]

The school was, of course, taken over under the later Acts and is now a controlled non-provided primary school with both boys and girls. Until 1905 it had only masters, but at the end of that year the first mistress was appointed and since then all the teachers have been women. The life of the school is now drawing to a close as a new primary school had just been built and opened in the neighbouring Grassington to which the Threshfield School children will before long be transferred. So will end a school which has served the area well for three centuries.

CHAPTER ELEVEN

A parish in 1851

To LOOK at a page of recently-printed census returns for a large administrative area is to see a mass of closely printed figures, twelve columns and about eighty lines of numbers to the page. Some hundreds of numbers are listed under a variety of headings – acreage of the townships and districts, then many figures under the general heading of population, then more re-lating to private households and dwellings. To these summary figures can be added a vastly greater number published in the analytical volumes for the counties and in the reports of the Registrar-General. It would seem, at first looking into them, that there is such a mass of figures as no one but a mathematician could use, but however dull these assemblies of numbers may seem, they can be made to tell a story of human activities and social conditions and to give the materials for a picture of the life of a community at a particular time and place.

The first census was taken in 1801 and then every ten years after, but not until 1841 were the returns anything but purely numerical. The 1841 census was taken on June 7th and this time every individual was not only counted but was recorded by his or her full name and the ages were placed in five-year groups. For example, an age of 30 merely meant that the person was 30, 31, 32, 33 or 34 years of age. This enumeration also answered the question whether the persons were born within the county in which they were living, with a plain 'yes' or 'no'. However, the census taken on March 30th, 1851, was recorded in far more detail. It gives the full names, exact age, the head of each household, the sex and relationship of all the members, and the living and working conditions of the popula-tion. The parish and county in which each person was born, wherever it was, and the number of houses and size of families and occupations of all persons are listed. Thus for the first time a lot of information of interest to the social historian became available and a true picture of the population in any area could be built on a basis of precise and accurate statistics.

A journey of nine miles by road to the north of Skipton takes one to Grassington, the best known and principal village in the upper part of neighbouring Wharfedale. Grassington is only one of the four townships which together make up the ecclesiastical parish of Linton. It is a characteristic of the dales parishes that they are of wide extent, with several, even in one case as many as eighteen, townships (villages, now civil parishes) within their bounds. The townships of Linton parish are Grassington and Hebden on the north-east side of the river and Linton and Threshfield on the south-west. We will take Linton parish as our example and see what we can learn from the census returns of 1851.

There is one ancient stone bridge over the River Wharfe, Linton Bridge (though now almost universally called Grassington Bridge), connecting the two parts of the parish between Grassington and Threshfield, and there is a footbridge, now of steel lattice but for a long time only of timber. This was built to make a footway between Grassington and Linton Mill when the mill was turned over to textiles at the turn of the nineteenth century. The stone bridge was built in 1603 to replace a timber one which for some years had been derelict from the action of serious floods, to the annoyance of travellers and the danger of local people who used it to get to and from the church. The whole cost of building the bridge was met by the West Riding, and though most other bridges over the River Wharfe have been broken at one time or another by subsequent floods, this bridge has stood undamaged. The downstream part of it is the original ribbed-arch portion and the plain upstream part is an eighteenth-century widening. The parish church stands away from all the villages, in a bend of the river very nearly central to them all, and near the church there are stepping-stones across the river for the convenience of the Hebden folk (Fig 14).

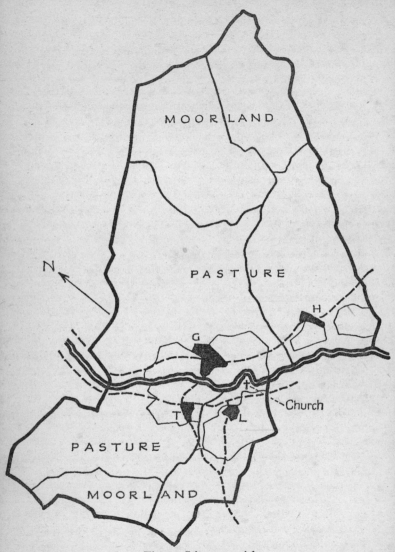

Fig 14. Linton parish

The parish stretches for 4 miles along the river, the centre of which is the boundary between the townships of Linton and Threshfield on one side and Grassington and Hebden on the other. From the river at 500 ft OD level it is 5½ miles to the watershed boundary of Grassington and Hebden, which runs along the moors at about 1,800 ft OD between Wharfedale and Nidderdale. The boundary of Threshfield and Linton is only 2 miles from the river and only reaches a height of about 1,200 ft OD. The villages all stand away from the river on side streams. Linton and Threshfield are on the western end of a large glacial moraine which here crosses the valley, so that they stand on a gravel ridge about 100 ft above the river on becks which breach the moraine. Grassington, across the river, is on the other end of the same moraine about a mile away. The moraine surface is between 600 ft and 700 ft OD. Hebden is on Hebden Beck, ½ mile from the river.

There is a broad shallow valley through the hills to the south of Linton communicating with Airedale, and through this valley the road and railway (now closed except for goods traffic) connects the upper dale with Skipton. In 1853 this road was made into a turnpike to replace a branch of it which for eighty years had connected Grassington with the Leeds and Liverpool Canal at Gargrave. There are two turnpikes which cross the parish. One is from Pateley Bridge in Nidderdale to Grassington (see Chapter Seven, p 116) and this part of a very old road continues up the dale to Kettlewell where it joins the other turnpike. This other road, on the south-west side of the river, was made in the latter part of the eighteenth century to improve and connect several old lengths of road into the new Addingham to Askrigg turnpike. These three roads are the classified road connexions with Linton parish and the outside world.

In the nineteenth century Linton parish offered three principal occupations: farming, mining and textiles. The farmland consisted of the old open fields near the river and on the moraine, long ago enclosed by agreement and used as meadow for hay production and stock-rearing with some dairy farming. The common pastures were given over mainly to young stock feeding and are on a belt of natural limestone pasture ranging up the fellsides to about 1,000 ft OD where the Millstone Grit brings in the rougher grasses, sedges and heather moors. These moors are stinted sheep pastures on which, taken together for the whole parish, several thousand sheep are run. On the higher part of the common pastures and the lower part of the moors a broad belt of mineral veins crosses Grassington and Hebden townships and forms what is generally known as the Grassington Moor mining field. The textile mills are on the riverside at Linton and Grassington and on Hebden Beck a few hundred yards away from the river. There were cornmills at Threshfield near the junction of a tributary stream with the river and just across that stream from Linton Mill, and also at Hebden, adjoining the textile mill.

Looking first at the population in general terms, throughout the dales area the nineteenth century saw a rise to a maximum about the middle years of the century and then a steady decline to its lowest level about 1891. The rise was not due to one cause only. The local mines, after a certain amount of stag-

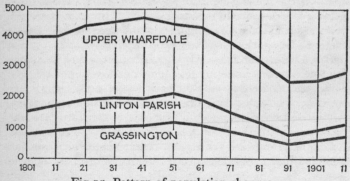

Fig 15. Pattern of population changes

nation, had expanded between 1800 and 1830; then, soon after 1850, they declined sharply and after 1860 the principal mines closed down, leaving only a few very small companies to struggle on. The textiles, which had likewise expanded from about 1790 and, in fact, had taken over many old cornmills (see Chapter Six), expanded for a few decades, but with the development of steam power the move to the new mills nearer to the fuel supplies which came from the coalfields by canal led to the closure of nearly all the smaller mills soon after the mid-century. The diagram (Fig 15) shows this pattern of population changes and it is clear that Grassington township, Linton parish and the whole upper dale all follow the same pattern. The lowest ebb of population was from about 1890 to 1895 and then the tourists began to come and some of them to settle, a movement which was accelerated by the opening of the Yorkshire Dales Railway to Threshfield in 1901. With this rise in interest many of the empty miners' cottages were bought (often for a mere £5) and improved, and rows of houses were built for men then working in Bradford offices. They could travel to and from Bradford by the local train, which connected at Skipton with 'the businessman's express' morning and evening.

The census of 1851 shows us the dale at the mid-point of the nineteenth century and probably the highest point of its prosperity. Let us look first at the relative sizes of the villages in Linton parish. There were 1,138 people living in Grassington, 460 in Hebden, 352 in Linton and 271 in Threshfield, so Grassington had more than half the population of the parish. It also had the largest area of township land, 5,806 acres; Hebden had 3,582 acres, Threshfield 2,648 acres and Linton only 1,282 acres. The dominance of Grassington in population and importance had been acquired at an early date, 1282, when Grassington was granted a charter for a market and a fair. The market shared with Kettlewell all the trade of the twenty miles of the upper dale. The opening and rapid expansion of the mines on Grassington Moor in the seventeenth century were accompanied by the immigration of families of miners from Swaledale and Derbyshire, who found some accommodation in tiny cottages made by the alteration of outhouses or by the division of larger houses. A great deal of the increase in the nineteenth-century population was housed in small cottages built as infilling in the many 'folds' which are characteristic of Grassington, running back from the main street in what were formerly long gardens.

Threshfield and Linton were unaffected by this phase of in-filling, and in fact there was practically none in the nineteenth century except for a row of cottages built adjacent to Linton Mill to house mill workers. This group of houses soon had the name of Botany which is still used. The name arose either in reference to Botany Bay, the inhabitants being exiled from the village of Linton, or to Botany wool, which was coming into the local textiles when the cottages were built.

As farming is the oldest occupation in the dales and still occupies an important place, long after the disappearance of mining and textiles, we will look first at that section of the community. The total number engaged in agriculture in one form or another was 199, and among these were 87 farmers the size of whose farms is stated, and 87 labourers including farmers' sons. Of the 87 farmers, 57 combined farming with some other job and for many of these the farm was in fact a smallholding or even less; 30 of them had farms of less than 10 acres and 12 of these had less than 5 acres, some as little as only 2 acres. Of all the farmers, 35 had farms between 10 and 50 acres and 13 had more than 100 acres. The pattern of farming in the dale was primarily based upon stock-rearing and feeding and this is clearly reflected in the land assessment returns made for the tithe commutation awards little more than ten years before our census date.

	Arable Acres	Meadow Acres	Pasture Acres	Moor Acres	Waste & Wood Acres
Linton	12	150	801	210	27
Threshfield	35	474	1314	589	229
Grassington	29	623	2772	2000	290
Hebden	30	350	518	2647	37

(Hebden Moor was inclosed by an Act of 1857)

Rilston	5	2095	849	101
Hetton	16	1982	100	2
Cracoe	10	1354	1000	6
Conistone	6	2500	2500	10

The arable was nearly all held by the larger farms and the medium and small farms were held in very small enclosures. This is seen in the tithe award schedules where, for example, a farm of 30 acres has 11 fields and 4 small crofts, or one of the large farms of 70 acres holds 19 fields and several small crofts.

The farmers who combined their land with another job are mainly miners (12), innkeepers (7) and carriers (8), with a variety of craftsmen – blacksmith (4), stonemason (2), wool comber (2), carpenter, shoemaker, clogger, cattle dealer (2), mine agent, butter factor, and so on. To these men the small piece of ground they occupied was supplementary to their regular work. It was just enough to allow a cow to be kept, to run a pig or some poultry, or to pasture and provide some winter hay for a pony or horse, and so help a poor wage with a small income; also, in many cases, it carried a few rights on the common pastures and moor which were of value.

The persons listed as in some form of textile work were divided between three mills, although these are not separately named, and between two branches of the industry which are usually indicated: worsteds and cotton. The worsteds had been manufactured at Linton Mill and at Grassington Low Mill, both established by the Birkbecks about 1790 to spin worsted yarns for the knitting industry of the dales. In 1851 Linton Mill was in the possession of two brothers, John and Francis Wall, who had succeeded W. & J. Birkbeck & Co in the 1840s. The Wall brothers had introduced power-loom weaving and with that and the spinning processes were largely producing Orleans – a plain cloth with a thin cotton warp and a worsted weft, involving both cotton and wool spinning, wool sorting and combing, and cotton-warp dressing. Many of the women were described as 'power-loom weaver (worsted and cotton)' and others as 'power-loom weaver, Orleans'. At Hebden Mill also the work was mixed, there being both cotton and yarn spinners and power-loom weavers, many specified as 'cotton and worsted'.

Of the 409 employees in textiles, 156 were men and 253 women, the women being the bulk of the weavers and spinners and the men being overlookers, wool sorters and combers, and

warp dressers. Boys and girls normally started at the age of
10 but a few started at 8, serving the spinners. The majority
of the women were between 11 and 20, with a smaller number
between 21 and 28 and very few above this age, though one or
two single women worked on into their 60s. The men were of a
more even age spread, though 10 to 20 was still slightly the
more frequent age. The age distribution, combined with
information gleaned from the parish registers, makes it clear
that it was normal for the girls of the parish who were not
kept at home to help in the house or on the farm to go to the
mill direct from school at 8 or 10 and to stay there until they
married. This employment for girls enabled families to supplement the miserable wages of the miners and labourers and
made it possible for a family with one or two daughters to
survive on a farm of 5 to 15 acres. In 1869 Bailey J. Harker
could write of Linton Mill:

> the mill is worked by water power, and was originally built
> for the manufacture of worsteds, but has been changed by
> the present owners to a cotton mill. About seventeen years
> ago (that would be 1852) it was great boon to the neighbour-
> hood, a large number of 'hands' being employed and good
> wages given, but now, not employing so many hands it
> would be almost as well without it.

The mining population can be counted in more ways than
one, depending on how many of the ancillary occupations we
include in the count. There are, for instance, blacksmiths
working at the mines, and carriers almost entirely employed
in carrying ore to the smelt mill, taking smelted lead to the
canal wharf at Skipton and returning with coal, timber and
stores for the mines. If, however, we make the simplest count
we have 157 miners, mostly working underground except for a
few boys on the dressing floors, 32 ore dressers on the surface,
11 smelters and 3 agents. All but about a dozen of the miners
lived in Grassington and Hebden and helped to give a character to these villages very different from that of Linton and
Threshfield, which remained rural villages with their greens

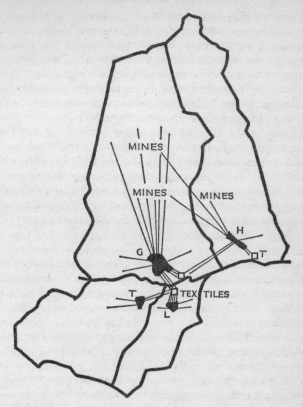

Fig 16. Movement to work. Each line represents twenty-five workers

and farms and farm buildings as the dominant features. None the less Linton and Threshfield gave shelter to many textile workers (Fig 16).

The mining population was all male, and as mining is almost always a lifelong occupation there was little movement from it. Boys started at the age of ten years, usually on the dressing floor and at the top of the shafts, and worked there for a time before going down into the mine. The mixed rock and ore sent up the shaft was hand-picked by boys and partly crushed by hand, and when it went forward to other stages of dressing it was generally a boy's job to move it and to serve the apparatus in which it was treated. When the boys went underground in their teens it was usually with father, brother or uncle, to be trained by them in the whole art and tradition of mining. In this way mining was very much a family occupation and in the census returns there are many families with the father and all his sons recorded as 'lead miner'. Of the miners, 140 were between the ages of 9 and 32 with no particular age after 12 dominating, but with six or seven men of each age. From 33 to 45 there are 38 miners, two or three for each year, then from 46 onwards the remaining 41 are spread unevenly and include men of 72, 78 and 81. From sources other than the census it appears that a few men in their forties left the underground work, either to go on to the dressing floors or to move to some other job away from the area. Most of these changes, which are to be seen in other fields as well, would follow the threat or onset of chest complaints due to the work in a confined air, powder fumes, ladder work and wet, which made mining conditions almost intolerable at times.

Farming, mining and textiles account for three-quarters of the occupied persons, the remaining quarter following a great variety of work in trade and services. A small professional group include a surgeon and a medical practitioner, five schoolmasters and five ministers of religion. On the fringe of the professional group is William Deville, theatre manager, and Jane Cataline, Professor of Music, both lodgers at the Black Horse Inn. They were from Hackney and Bethnal Green, and would be at the little theatre opened in Grassington by one Tom Airey. In 1808 he had a small company with which Edmund Kean and Harriet Mellor (later the Duchess of St Albans) acted. The theatre lapsed about the mid-1830s and this would be one of the several attempts made for its revival, Deville and Cataline being marked as temporary visitors.

Of the craftsmen the sixteen shoemakers, cloggers or cord-

wainers were kept busy by the miners and millhands for whom
strong boots and clogs were an essential, and by the harness
demands of the carriers. Blacksmiths and carpenters were employed about the mines and the mill, and the remainder were
the normal run of shopkeepers, dressmakers and tailors,
joiners and so on. A few may sound old-fashioned to our ears
but reflect a little country market village – hawker, cattle
drover, lime burner, washerwoman (and two who preferred to
be 'laundress'), Irish lodging-house keeper, and several
'errand girls'. These latter, along with eight bread bakers,
may reflect something of a condition found in the mill towns
where young married women went out to work and so needed
'errand girls' who would do their shopping and found bread
bakers to be a great convenience. Most Yorkshire wives
baked their own bread at home, but there were some small
cottages in Grassington without a good oven. In the neighbouring village of Conistone there was a bread baker, and a
notice, written down by the local bellman to be called and given
out by him, serves both to remind us of the baker and to
provide a fine specimen of the local dialect in the year 1839.

I am to give notige that Jennie Pickersgill yeats yewn to
neit, to moarn at mearn, and to moarne at neit, an' nea
langer, as lang as storme hods, cos he can git na mare eldin.

He gives notice that Jennie is without firewood because of the
storm, and so will only heat her oven 'tonight, tomorrow
morning and tomorrow night'. This suggests that Jennie's
oven was used by folks who prepared their own dough and that
she was literally a baker and a maker of bread.

One valuable feature of the 1851 census enumeration is the
inclusion of the age of each person along with his or her place
of birth. From this information we can learn much about the
movement of population, particularly if one makes an analysis
of the returns for a wide area such as Craven rather than for a
single parish. We can place more confidence in the figures of a
single parish when we find them repeating more general
patterns. The movement of families is very different from the

general idea, accepted by popular writers and the public, that most of the families in the dales villages have been unchanged for many generations or even for centuries. This is true of a few families whose names are in the parish register from its first pages in the sixteenth century, but they are not very many. There are even villages where the names of the 1851 census return have no representative whatever in the 1951 census, every family having changed during that hundred years. Again there are some family names which are now associated with villages and looked upon as being the original native stock, but which came from other areas only during the nineteenth century. The incoming and outgoing has been connected to a large extent with the pattern of work. Textiles and mining, which tempted families into the dales at different periods, were equally responsible by their decline and collapse for the migration of whole families away from the area. We can, therefore, best look at these movements first in the light of the two main industries, textiles and mining (Fig 17).

There are sixty-two textile workers, most of them with families, who moved into the area from other parts. Twenty-two families lived at Linton Mill, in the two rows of cottages built about the beginning of the century by the Birkbecks for their workpeople. One row was later demolished and a row of more modern houses built in its place; the other row has been modernized by bringing two cottages into one, so making a number of larger and more convenient houses. Of the incomers to the mill fourteen families came from Addingham twelve miles down the dale and an early centre of cotton spinning. Ten families came from the woollen areas around Halifax and Bradford, and the rest partly from the Lancashire and Yorkshire border area of cotton manufacture and partly from the worsted-spinning areas of the dales to the north-west, Aysgarth, Askrigg, Hawes, Garsdale and Dent. There are five families from the flax-spinning areas between Pateley Bridge and Knaresborough (see Chapter Six for these industries). One or two remaining families moved in from parts of upper Wharfedale. In the mixed worsted and cotton trade which developed here, men and women, boys and girls, could all find employment so we have, typically, whole families involved.

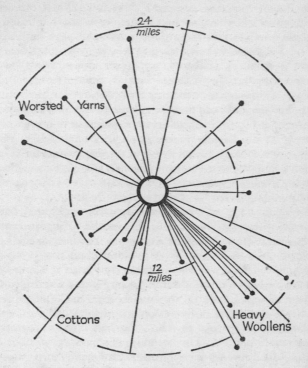

Fig 17. Textile workers coming to Linton

This census, with the ages and birthplaces of the people, offers a fine chance to study family histories, and one or two examples will throw a little light also on the structure of the industry. We will look first at the record of William Peckover, living at Linton Mill. He was 44, born in Long Preston, between Airedale and Wharfedale. His wife Olive, 43, was born in Barrowford, Lancashire, near the cotton town of Nelson. William was a cotton-warp dresser and was more likely to have learned this trade in Barrowford than in Long

Preston, so it may be that his parents moved there when he was a boy. His first child, James, was born in Barrowford and was 19 at the 1851 census. His next child was Ellin, 17 (power-loom weaver of Orleans in 1851), and she was born in Addingham, so William had moved there between 1832 and 1834. His next children were all born at Addingham: Elizabeth, 15 (worsted spinner), Rebecca, 13 (warp dresser's assistant), Spencer, 11 (warp dresser's assistant), Isabella, 8 (scholar), and John, 6 (scholar). This brings us down to 1845 for the birth of John, but the next child, Sarah Ann, 4, and Maria, 1, were both born at Linton Mill, so the family must have moved from Addingham to Linton about 1846–7. William, as a warp dresser, would only be following a general custom in taking Rebecca and Spencer into the mill at 11 or 12 to work with him as 'dresser's assistants' until Rebecca could become a weaver or spinner and Spencer a warp dresser.

We might look at another family with a different background – that of William Gill, lead miner, living at Linton Mill in 1851. He was born at Kettlewell, 10 miles up the dale, 50 years old and a widower. His eldest child was Ellin, 21, now a power-loom weaver at Linton, but born at Kettlewell, as were his next four children, his sons John, 19, and George, 17, lead miners, Sarah, 13, his housekeeper, and William, 10, a spinner and scholar. William was one of the small number of 'half-timers' who went to school for half a day and worked half a day in the mill. The last child Margaret, 5, was born at Linton Mill. Here we have a lead miner's family in Kettlewell until between 1841 and 1846 when they moved to Linton. The two elder boys followed their father into the mines but the elder daughter went into the mill. The mines, following the depression of 1839, were almost stagnant in Kettlewell until 1863, and the small cotton mill was closed. With a period of prosperity in the Grassington Moor mines and the new management at Linton Mill, there was every inducement for the family to move, as we have seen they did.

There were some families, however, who had nearly all been born in Linton parish, as for instance John Irving, 46, a wool comber who was born in Gargrave but married his wife,

Margaret, at Linton. She was born in Grassington and it seems likeliest that John had come to work at Linton Mill, met his wife probably as a young woman in the mill, and settled down there. Their children, William, 21, wool comber like his father, Richard, 19, Isabella, 17, Margaret, 16, John, 14, James, 12, and Bell, 10, all worked in the spinning shed, and his two youngest, Mary Ellin, scholar, and Alice, were 6 and 4.

The majority of families which moved into the parish to work at the mill appear to have done so about 1846, when the brothers, John and Francis Wall, moved from Addingham and took Linton Mill. Hebden is very different from Linton, the workers at its mill being nearly all Hebden born and very few moving in from outside. It was common for the boys in Hebden to get work at the mines and the girls at the mill, and this, with the fact that the mill had been established for more than a generation, seems to have produced a more stable community than at Linton, where the mill had declined and had then been revived on a new kind of work about 1846.

The family pattern of the farmers is, as one would expect, markedly different from both mining and textiles. A much larger proportion of the farmers have moved no farther than from some neighbouring village in the same dale and many are in the village where they were born. Among the farm men who are married, man and wife are very commonly from different villages with one of them in the village where he or she was born and the other from a village still within the dales. With the check of the parish registers to help out, one sees that what usually happens is that in a farmer's family the son either stays at home on a moderate-sized farm or goes away as a labourer on some other farm. He either marries a girl who has come as farm servant or a daughter on the farm where he works. In a chance group of farmers' families taken from the Linton census, Linton-born farmers married wives from Aysgarth, Halton Gill, Pateley Bridge and Wensleydale, and others married and moved to the birthplaces of wives in Litton, Coverdale, Waygill and Askrigg, and so on. The movement would appear to be unmarried men and women going into farm service, probably through the hiring fairs or through contacts made by parents at the markets, and then marrying and settling down in the village to which they have gone. By studying the census returns for ten different townships in other parts of the dales this pattern becomes very clear.

With time it would be possible to make a valuable analysis of the families and the housing in the villages, and this could to a large extent be correlated with the actual buildings, as not many have been destroyed. Some of the smaller miners' cottages have been thrown two into one or even three into one, as many of them were of the tiny 'one up – one down' variety. However, for a general statement, the census lists 465 houses with 2,221 people living in them, an average of just less than five persons per house. Men and women are very evenly balanced, 1,114 men and 1,107 women. Among the families three children seem to be a fairly common number, but there are a few larger groups. In one house there were husband and wife (43 and 42), six children and the wife's sister, the children ranging from 17 to 3 years. In another a man and wife, both 49, had eight children, 22 to 5, and one house held man and wife, a servant and nine children. Occasionally the family includes near relations, generally those who have come to work in the mill – man and wife, three children, two sisters-in-law, one brother-in-law, and two nephews; all except an infant and a lead miner worked at the mill. The larger families are mostly among the textile workers. One mill family has nine children and eight of the family work in the mill, only the wife and an infant being at home. On the whole, the farmers have the smaller families. There is no doubt, however, that among the textile workers and the miners there was a large number of badly overcrowded houses.

CHAPTER TWELVE

Discovering the dales

THE DISCOVERY of the Yorkshire dales as an area to be visited and enjoyed by ordinary folk is a matter of the last hundred years, though in some aspects they were becoming known to a few in the early years of last century. During the eighteenth century there were many people travelling about the country, writing journals of their tours and making comments on what they saw. At the same time a race of local and county historians was emerging who produced histories of towns or areas on a new scale of detail. Artists were producing portfolios of new scenes and Gilpin was discoursing on 'picturesque beauty', particularly of mountains, lakes and trees. None of the travellers and artists, however, made close acquaintance with the fells – they were a useful background in Gilpin's ideal compositions, in certain circumstances, but they had elements of terror and horror which forbade too close an exploration. They were to be seen from carefully selected viewpoints and a correctly balanced scene was to be looked for into which they would fit. In fact, many early travellers regarded the whole area of the dales as wild mountainous country. Defoe in 1724 had come in his tour through England as far as the Yorkshire dales, but records in his journal that:

Here [Skipton] we turned north-west which brought us to a place called Settle, a much better town than we expected in such a country. It lies upon the road to Lancaster at the foot of the mountains that part that county from Yorkshire upon the river Ribble. Looking forward to the north-west of us we saw nothing but high mountains, which had a

terrible aspect and more frightful than any in Monmouth-
shire or Derbyshire, especially Penigent Hill. So that having
no manner of inclination to encounter them, merely for the
sake of seeing a few villages and a parcel of wild people,
we turned short north-east and came ... to a village called
Burnsall.

Bray in 1777 was one early traveller who ventured into
Wensleydale, then by Wharfedale and Malham came to
Skipton. He could speak of Jervaulx and Coverham abbeys,
Middleham and Bolton castles and the waterfalls around
Aysgarth and Askrigg with enthusiasm, but going up Bishopdale
to get into Wharfedale he can only say 'at the end of Bishop's-
dale, come out on a wild dreary moor, and ascend a long steep
hill, on the top of which are some black and dismal peat
mosses'. In the years following Bray's tour many travellers
visited Yorkshire, but with few exceptions they confined their
journeys to the main road on the east of the Pennines, passing
through Wakefield, Leeds, Ripon and so to Richmond, none
of them making a diversion into the dales which lie to the west
of this road. A few travellers went by the Keighley to Kendal
turnpike road, which goes through Settle, Ingleton and Kirkby
Lonsdale, on their way to the Lake District and, of these, John
Hutton in 1780 stayed at Settle and Ingleton to visit the
caves there. He says in the introduction to his *Guide to the
Lakes*:

the amusement you have received in visiting the natural
curiosities of Ingleton and Settle in company with different
parties of gentlemen of approved taste and knowledge, who
entertained the same sentiments with yourself, hath induced
me to draw up a plain narrative of one of our excursions, in
a letter to a friend by way of an appendix to the Guide to
the Lakes.

This letter runs to one hundred pages and is the first account
that is almost a step by step guide to the area around Ingleborough, Settle and Malham. A few years later, in 1786,

Hurtley, the schoolmaster of Malham, published his *Concise Account of Some Natural Curiosities in the Environs of Malham* and these were indeed the 'natural curiosities' which Hutton had visited.

In the later years of the eighteenth century and the early years of the nineteenth, the emphasis remained on 'natural curiosities' and travellers diverged from the main roads into the wilder parts only to visit and admire these already known 'curiosities'. At the same time artists were looking for the picturesque and romantic and a few were exploring the better-known parts of the dales. The general countryside, however, was unnoticed and was seen only occasionally as a background within which there were rocks and waterfalls, wooded gorges, ivy-grown ruins, and caves to be visited and sketched. The normal view of a beautiful countryside was one well cultivated with trim hedges and well-placed plantations, set with 'gentlemen's seats' which were the reference points on all journeys. The early maps marked all the parks and the road books drew attention to the gentlemen's seats on each hand of the journey. The information printed alongside the road details gives

Bingley. *St Ives*, Edward Ferrand Esq; *Myrtle Grove*, Gen Twiss; and *Harden Grange*, Walker Ferrand Esq. Keighley, 1 mile before, *Riddlesden Hall*, W. Slingsby Esq; Steeton, *Steeton Hall*, Christopher Netherwood Jun. Esq,

and so on all the way across the country.[1]

A change is noticeable with the visits of Turner and Girtin to the north at the turn of the century. Both had visited lower Wharfedale and penetrated as far as Bolton Priory, and had also gone as far as Malham to see the Gordale Scar and the Cove. In his sketch-books Turner has drawings of Settle and Skipton, and others which show that he was exploring these parts on more than one occasion. When Thomas Dunham Whitaker planned his *History of Whalley* and later his *History of Yorkshire*, he was put in touch with Turner, whom he employed to illustrate his 'Whalley' and his 'Richmondshire'.

For these Turner, particularly for Richmondshire, was compelled to wander through the dales, of which Wensleydale, Swaledale and part of the Greta and Tees valleys lie within Richmondshire. His many drawings, while including monastic ruins, also include wider views of the countryside and lead away from the 'natural curiosities' to the true landscapes.

About the middle years of the nineteenth century another change appears, when notice begins to be taken of the dales as an area of country in which walking can provide a profitable recreation and the countryside can afford a great variety of interest – botanical, historical and scenic. Two factors seem to have contributed to this new view of the country. The railways, which were then being made, opened up new stretches of country as Howson in a little guide to Craven says in 1850:

and now, not only the man of leisure and wealth, but the imprisoned denizen of the crowded town, and the toiling artizan will be enabled to visit these attractive places, for the new-constructed railways, though they may encroach a little upon the retirement and pastoral character of the country, offer a facility of transit which even the pedestrian is sometimes glad to avail himself of, and a cheapness and speed of which the poor in money or in time may reap the benefit.

His guide describes the country and recommends several walking routes, often of 10 to 14 miles, by which it can best be seen.

A very important influence on the development of outdoor exploration and of walking was the growth of the Mechanics' Institutes. The founder of the movement, Dr George Birkbeck, was born in Settle and educated first at the little Quaker school at Newton in Bolland (of which school John Bright was a pupil) then at Sedbergh School in north-west Yorkshire. He had little interest in games, but wandered widely about the countryside. In the Mechanics' Institutes which sprang from his work in Glasgow and London a keen interest in natural science was developed, and as Institutes spread through the north from about 1830 great numbers of working men acquired a desire to know more of the countryside and its natural history.

Mechanics' Institutes had been formed before 1850 in Skipton, Settle (1831) and Richmond on the fringe of the dales, and in many towns of the industrial areas of Yorkshire and east Lancashire. Local naturalist and antiquarian societies also appeared about this time and many of them arranged indoor winter meetings for lectures and, in the lighter summer evenings and at weekends, outdoor 'rambles' to search the countryside to see its botanical treasures, hear its birds and even to study its geology.

By 1847 the railway was completed from Leeds to Skipton and the Lancashire and Yorkshire Railway and the Little North Western linked Skipton with Colne and much of Lancashire, and with Settle and Lancaster. It was these train services which made the dales accessible to the new groups of people with outdoor and naturalist interests. The new lines ran along the southern border of the dales, but to the north a line was constructed from Darlington (on the North Eastern) to Richmond, in 1846; this brought Swaledale within reach of the growing south Durham and Teesside population. In 1856 a branch line was made from the main line at Northallerton to Leyburn in Wensleydale. Thus it was possible to get from the industrial areas to the edges of the dale country. Innkeepers began to see a new business opportunity and some of them, in Grassington for instance, by 1860 were advertising their 'posting' facilities – trains could be met at Skipton and passengers carried to Grassington and, if desired, forwarded from there farther up the dale. Transport could also be hired from Settle and Richmond, so that excursions well into the dales became possible.

Two books show the impact of this new desire for 'rambling' on foot. The first, by William Dobson in 1864, had the title *Rambles by the Ribble*. These are very detailed accounts of actual walks and walking tours taken in Ribblesdale from the source of the river down to Clitheroe, with some diversions

across to Malham. The sketches had appeared in the *Preston
Chronicle* and their reprinting in a handy form which would
serve as a guide to the actual walks was the result of a widespread demand. Dobson and the companion with whom he
walked made good use of the railway:

> We left Preston for Lancaster by train, and thence went to
> Bentham by the 'Little North-Western' line, along the
> beautiful valley of the Lune ... We had got a lift from
> Bentham to Hill House (Inn) in the landlord's 'white-
> chapel'.

The Hill Inn was seven miles from Bentham and it was a
common practice of many of the walkers to go by rail to some
point, stay overnight and, with a very early start next morning
get well on the way by carriage for the walking part. The
accounts of the walks are full of excellent detail and description
and have very full notes of the botany in which the two walkers
took a great interest. Some of the larger fells were climbed,
Ingleborough summit being visited on the first day, and along
with the beauty and extent of the views the travellers had
great joy in seeing the cloud berry in fruit along with other
rarities.

In 1869 a comparable work appeared, *Rambles in Upper
Wharfedale*, written by Bailey J. Harker. Harker starts by
saying that the approach to the dale will be by train to Skipton
and in a brief appendix says that

> post horses may be had in Grassington of Mr Thomas
> Septimus Airey, so called from being Old Tom Airey's
> seventh son. Mr Airey also runs several Omnibuses every
> day from Grassington to Skipton and vice versa in time
> for the trains to and from Leeds, Bradford, Manchester
> and Lancaster.

There is also a conveyance each day to and from Skipton,
Kettlewell and Hebden. Harker includes in his *Rambles* a
fair amount of local history, much of which proves now

to be valuable contemporary comment, but his rambling
is largely confined to the direct roads between village and
village, with few diversions except to natural features such
as the limestone gorge of Trollers Gill near Skyreholm and
the Stump Cross Caverns on the Pateley road. None the
less it is full of information and its 290 pages are still read
by the visitors and natives lucky enough to get hold of a
copy.

Nidderdale had its careful historian in William Grainge,
who in 1863 produced his *Nidderdale; An Historical, Topo-
graphical and Descriptive Sketch of the Valley of the Nidd.*
This was printed by Thomas Thorpe of Pateley Bridge, and
Grainge says that Thorpe took pride in the fact that this was
the first book ever printed in Nidderdale. In its preface the
book is described as a 'guide to the pleasure-seeking tourist'
and is so arranged that from Pateley Bridge as a centre the
whole valley could be visited in four one-day tours (Illus. 26).
The railway from the North Eastern line at Nidd to Pateley
Bridge was opened May 1st, 1862, and was expected to
'induce many to visit the district who would not otherwise
have done so'. The book is of great merit and gives sufficient
room to the local industries, institutions and population to
make it of great value to the social and economic historian.
An indication of the recognition of the tourist trade is found
in the few pages of advertising matter where, for instance, the
Crown Inn at Pateley Bridge 'has every accommodation for
Parties Visiting Pateley Bridge, Stump Cross Caverns, Brimham Rocks etc' and 'Day Parties will find every attention paid
to their comfort'. Other inns offer similar attention, and the
Unicorn Hotel and Posting House promises omnibuses,
broughams, open carriages, cabs, gigs, phaetons, and conveyances of every description, for parties visiting all parts
of the dale (Fig 18).

Pateley Bridge was the earliest of the dales towns to appeal
to the new breed of 'tourists' as such and to offer particular
attractions to be seen on the payment of a small entrance fee
(see Fig 18). An advertisement for Brimham Rocks shows a
new trend in catering. After stating that the entrance fee is

6*d* (2½p) and the rocks are not to be seen on Sundays, the advertisement goes on:

> Richard Weatherhead, Brimham House, accommodates Parties with Tea, Coffee, Lemonade, Ginger Beer, Soda Water, etc. on the shortest notice.
>
> TO VISITORS BY RAIL – As the railway is now open to Dacre Banks Station the nearest point to Brimham Rocks, R. W. respectfully informs the numerous visitors they can have Plates, Dishes and Crockery of all kinds provided on reasonable terms, for those who bring their own refreshments.
>
> The Roads have been recently improved.

In the more northerly dales there were no comparable guidebooks to these three and it was not until the railway was completed from Leyburn to Hawes in 1877 that Wensleydale awoke to its tourist potential. Visitors began to explore its main features, but the great inrush was begun in 1885 at Hardraw Scar. This is a magnificent waterfall near the foot of Fossdale, not far from the river and opposite Hawes, about a mile from the railway station. In 1885 a band contest was organized in the wider part of the lovely ravine leading up to the fall. Brass bands were a great feature of these dales and almost every village had its band and its 'band room' where practices were held. This first contest was so successful, with bands both from Wensleydale and Swaledale and a great crowd to hear them, that it was made an annual event. Thousands of people came to the contests and excursion trains crowded the line between Hawes, Garsdale Junction and Northallerton Junction. Wagonettes did a great trade carrying people across to Hardraw on these occasions, and caterers were usually eaten out of stock before the end of the day. Although the contests ceased after a while, the tradition of going to Hardraw persisted and it still remains a popular place for tourists. For a time, about the turn of the century, choir contests took the place of the band events and were equally popular.

TO TOURISTS
AND OTHERS,
VISITING PATELEY BRIDGE
AND THE NEIGHBOURHOOD.

THE
FISHPOND, RAVENSGILL, AND GUY'S-CLIFFE WOODS,
Belonging to JOHN YORKE, ESQ., BEWERLEY HALL,

WILL BE

OPEN
ON TUESDAYS AND THURSDAYS
ONLY,

Between 9 a.m., and 6 p.m., on Payment of

SIXPENCE EACH.

Tickets and Guide to be had of Mr. DAVID PARKINSON, Bewerley.

SCHOOLS WILL BE
ADMITTED AT REDUCED RATES,

ON APPLICATION BEING MADE TO

MR. WARWICK,
AGENT TO JOHN YORKE, ESQ.

☞ *TO COMMENCE 5TH OF MAY.*

For a description of Ravensgill, Guy's-cliffe, Stump Cross Caverns, Stean Beck, Goydon Pot Hole, &c., see "History of Nidderdale," published by T. Thorpe, Pateley Bridge.

Fig 18. Advertisement from Grainge's 'Nidderdale', 1863

T–G

The railway from Settle to Carlisle by Ribblehead was completed in 1876 and this, with stations right in the heart of the Pennines, brought new areas within reach of the tourist and walker. *A Guide to the District of Craven and the Settle and Carlisle Railway* quickly appeared and described an abundance of walks and tours based upon the line. In its advertising pages one gets again a glimpse of how the district adapted itself to the new traffic. Mr John Kilburn advertised that he had 'built a house specially for the accommodation of visitors to this romantic and secluded part of the district' near to the railway station at Ribblehead. The New Inn at Clapham was recently 'enlarged and improved' and at Ingleton the Ingleborough Hotel was a 'new and stately erection' fitted in every way to suit visitors and families coming for health or pleasure. A guide to the caves, etc, around Ingleton and Clapham appeared, and a few professional guides to the caves gave the terms for their services. The tourist trade was established now in its own right.

From these beginnings it developed slowly, and near the end of the century was helped by the writings of a historian, Harry Speight of Bingley, who between 1891 and 1902 wrote a series of large books on the various dales: *From Goole to Malham in Airedale*, 1891; *Craven and the north-west Yorkshire Highlands*, 1892; *Nidderdale*, 1894; *Romantic Richmondshire*, 1897; *Upper Wharfedale*, 1900; and *Lower Wharfedale*, 1902. These covered all the dales and used Whitaker's histories as a basis, with the addition of some new material from the public records. They proceeded systematically up each dale, village by village, and with a true Victorian flavour were concerned with the manor house and the church, but in addition gave notice to antiquities and to interesting sidelights of history and local characters. They became very popular and aroused a widespread interest in the dales. A few years later Edmund Bogg of Leeds gathered round him a group of young artists with enthusiasm for the dales, and, in various groups, they accompanied Bogg in tramps and walking tours over practically all the ground which Speight had disclosed. Bogg's volumes describing these tours are much less formal than

Speight's, much more romantic, and include ballads, legends, memories of old people, and, though far less accurate and careful, they appealed to a wide public. Many a youth has been drawn to the dales through the influence of Bogg and the charming illustrative sketches provided by his artist group. Also cheap shilling editions were produced which included the best of his larger writing.

We can say then that by the opening of the twentieth century the dales had been discovered by the tourist, accommodation was being provided for him, and books to guide his steps were available. However, the walker still walked along the roads and lanes and only ventured occasionally on to the footpaths and the open fells. In 1890 Bailey J. Harker had returned to Grassington from many years away as a Congregational minister, and he produced a new kind of guide. He called it *The Buxton of Yorkshire* and wrote about Wharfedale, with a major section on 'Its various Walks'. This was indeed a footpath guide to take people off the roads and on to some of the higher ground. Other 'Walks round . . .' types of guide appeared and the rambler had entered the dales. There was some opposition to the use of footpaths, and access to some areas was refused; it was this that brought on to the scene one of the outstanding 'characters' of the dales, John Crowther, herbalist and cow doctor, antiquary and footpath defender. He was born in Bradford in 1858, his father one of an old Bradford working family and his mother from Kettlewell, where her brother, Benjamin Ward, was village blacksmith, a skilled botanist and a friend of the schoolmaster Carradice of whom we have already written in Chapter Ten. After his elementary schooldays Crowther wished to become an apothecary, but there was not enough money available to pay the required premium for an apprenticeship. His father was a shoemaker and combined with this a small draper's shop in which the young Crowther served for some time, but without giving up his intention of being a herbalist. After a year or two he was delighted to be able to enter, as an assistant, the shop of Dr Tempest which was known as the 'Bradford Botanic Dispensary'. J. Tempest, MD, MB, MRA, described himself as 'botanic physician and surgeon', and urged people needing 'more efficacious treatment than the one they have already had' to try his. No one, he says, ever regrets having done so.[2]

After a few years with Dr Tempest, during which he was enabled to place his interest in herbs on a very sound basis and to learn the rudiments of dispensing, he moved to Grassington where, through the influence of his Uncle Benjamin, already a well-skilled herbalist, he was taken as an apprentice by Dr Anthony. This was in 1880 and he was soon serving in Dr Anthony's small dispensing shop. The doctor died in 1884 and Crowther was sufficiently advanced to take over the shop as his own and to give his name to the directories as chemist and druggist. For the rest of his working life this remained his occupation and means of livelihood. He had soon demonstrated while with Dr Anthony a considerable skill with animals, and while still a young man he became known throughout the dales as a good and reliable 'cow doctor' and was sent for from far and wide.

In his increasing practice as an animal doctor Crowther must have visited nearly every farm in the dale, often going from one farm to another by field paths or hill paths, even crossing occasionally into neighbouring dales. In this way he learned of the wealth of footpaths in the dale and at the same time saw the large number which were in danger of being lost through disuse or obstruction. It was not long before he started noting the footpaths on his maps, walking them and protesting against obstructions. In particular, a fine riverside walk on the south bank of the river between Threshfield and Kilnsey was obstructed by a landowner who secured an order from Quarter Sessions diverting it off his ground on to the highway. After 1902, when part of the land near the river was being developed for housing for the incoming Bradfordians, some of the new owners tried to stop paths across the bits of land of which they had, in their own minds, become lords and masters.

The agent of the Duke of Devonshire, fearing the increased numbers of working-class visitors which the new railway from Skipton to Grassington might bring, declared Grass Woods as private and all the footpaths in and through them to be no more than permissive paths. To establish this the woods were closed for one day each year and keepers and estate servants were placed on guard at all entrances. Grass Woods is one of the major attractions in upper Wharfedale, extending for over 260 acres from the riverside up to the heights of Bastow Wood at over 950 ft OD. It is a wood with many fine limestone scars and terraces, very rich in archaeological remains, and with an exceptionally rich and rare limestone flora. It lies only half a mile from Grassington and has been used for generations by Grassington people for recreation and for the collection of 'estovers' – dead wood for fuel and herbs for the pot.

During Christmas week, 1901, Crowther, his wife and two sons were prevented from entering the wood and told that it was private and closed. Others had the same experience, so in response a group of local people formed an informal association to defend their rights in the wood and also to look to rights of way in the whole area. Bailey Harker was a joint promoter of this with Crowther, and they had the enthusiastic support of Robert Carlisle and some other farmers. In 1902 parties were organized to walk every path in the Grass Woods on the closure day, and when stopped by woodmen and others at the various entrances gave their names and forced their way into the wood. All these events were reported in writing by the chief woodman, and these reports make some very interesting reading. The closing of the wood on a particular Sunday in each year continued until within the last few years, but the paths were walked by large numbers of people, except for one year when the Duke's agent changed the usual closure day and the crowds came a week late.

A path on the opposite side of the river was closed and its stiles walled up, but Crowther, with a large crowd of Grassington folk, unwalled the stiles and destroyed a number of notices forbidding the use of the path. The threat to rights of way caused Crowther to collect sworn affidavits from a number of older people, setting down their memories and usage of paths, and these affidavits were used to very good effect in footpath tribunals in 1965 and 1966. Crowther had a great interest in

THE YORKSHIRE DALES RAILWAY
(SKIPTON TO GRASSINGTON).

CUTTING of the FIRST SOD at the GRASSINGTON TERMINUS

On Thursday, June 7th, 1900,

By WALTER MORRISON, Esq., M.P.

Order of Procession for the Day.

Leave GRASSINGTON at One o'clock prompt in the following order:—

1. Children.
2. Grassington Brass Band.
3. Councillors, Overseers, and Public Officials.
4. General Public.

Arriving at THRESHFIELD at 1-30. Leave the Old Hall Inn at 1-45 prompt as follows, to the place of ceremony:—

1. Children.
2. Band.
3. Directors and Officials of the Yorkshire Dales Railway.
4. Clergy and other Ministers of Religion.
5. Parish, Rural, and Urban Councillors, Overseers of the Poor, and other Public Officials (including Schoolmasters).
6. General Public.

On arrival at the Field MR. W. A. PROCTER will hand Spade to MR. MORRISON.

MR. HUTCHINSON and MR. FERGUSON will hand Barrow to MR. MORRISON, and the latter gentleman will cut the sod.

COL. MAUDE will move, DR. WILKS second, and the REV. F. A. C. SHARE will support a Vote of Thanks to MR. MORRISON.

NATIONAL ANTHEM.

Procession will then reform, and proceed to Grassington.

Fig 19. Yorkshire Dales Railway

boys and formed a youth club, the Grassington Antiquarian and Footpath Society, which met weekly at his house and spent much time walking the paths and learning them for future reference, and also in listing antiquities and collecting flints and other things of interest.

Bailey Harker, in his *Buxton of Yorkshire*, had a chapter on the British forts and Roman camp which he claimed to have discovered near Grassington. Two years later he collected about £10 to excavate a burial mound in High Close Pasture, an excavation in which Crowther helped. This started a partnership in which Harker and Crowther recognized many prehistoric sites in the neighbourhood and explored them, though heavily obsessed with the idea that they were dealing largely with Roman remains when in fact they were discovering Iron Age and Romano-British field systems. Crowther was an untiring correspondent of the Bradford papers, and though his letters were usually brief they aroused a new interest in the area and brought many new visitors. Crowther began to sign himself 'Antiquary' and then 'Grassington Antiquary' and was able to interest people like Professor Boyd Dawkins of Manchester and some of the Council of the Yorkshire Geological Society who were interested in the excavations by Edward Jones, in the Elbolton Cave, only two miles away. As a result an Upper Wharfedale Exploration Committee was formed and some digging was done in Iron Age and Bronze Age barrows near Grassington, the remains from which were placed in two cases in the town hall. In 1902 the parish council asked Crowther to take charge of these remains and so gave him the desire to form a museum. In fact, a small museum was made in Crowther's own house, and after his retirement was moved into a hut which he built for it. This museum attracted many important archaeologists and became a well-known attraction. At his death the collection went to the Craven Museum, Skipton, where they are a valuable part of the exhibits.

In the excitement of archaeology the demands of botany were not overlooked, and a constant visitor to Crowther was Dr Druce, when revising Hayward's *Pocket Book of Botany*.

Many of Crowther's records appear in that book along with a hitherto unknown hybrid *Helleborine* which Druce named '*Crowtheri*'. For many years Crowther was well known as an authority on the Dales flora and his shop saw a constant stream of botanists as well as archaeologists, calling to seek his help or to view his herbarium. His contributions to the Press, along with a booklet he produced in 1920, *Rambles round Grassington*, added much to the popularity of the area, and there is no doubt that in the first decade of the century he gave an impetus to the scientific and archaeological visitors that led to upper Wharfedale becoming very widely known in a way not strictly paralleled in the other dales.

The most recent phase in the discovery of the dales has come with their designation in 1954 as the Yorkshire Dales National Park. This park includes all the portion of which we have been writing, with the exclusion only of Nidderdale. The very name National Park has brought an incessant stream of weekend motorists to look at it, and the opening of the Pennine Way along its western ridges, along with a rich sprinkling of youth hostels, has encouraged the younger visitors who are taking more interest in the higher fells and moors than the earlier visitors did. A new period of active discovery has started, and has brought with it problems for the dalesfolk and for the Park Planning Committee, none of which, however, will be incapable of happy solution.

CHAPTER THIRTEEN

Dentdale – the remote dale

ON THE length between Settle and Kirkby Stephen the Settle to Carlisle railway crosses the very head of Dentdale where Dent station, the highest in England, has a rail level of 1,145 ft above sea level. The station is 4 miles from the village of Dent, properly called Dent Town, and 700 ft above it. Four miles below Dent Town its river, the Dee, joins the Rawthey at a point about a mile below Sedbergh; in a farther mile and a half the Rawthey joins the Lune. This valley of Dentdale, only about 10 miles long, is remote from most of the bustle of the popular Yorkshire dales; it is tucked well away in the north-west corner of the West Riding 60 miles as the crow flies from Wakefield, the administrative centre, and, very much farther by road, is liable to be overlooked. Those people who really know Yorkshire, however, cherish this out-of-the-way, quiet place for its serene beauty, its people and its rich store of both legend and history. The surveyor for the Board of Agriculture in 1794 said 'we entered Dent dale from the west and proceeded down the dale to the town of Dent, which is nearly in the centre ... The whole dale is enclosed, and, viewed from the higher grounds, presents the picture of a terrestrial paradise'. No other part of the county is described in such glowing words.[1]

Today the curious railway passenger looking from the west side of the Thames-Clyde express, between Garsdale and Blea Moor tunnels, has for a few minutes the sensation of suspension hundreds of feet above a half-real scene. A deep valley stretching away between high fells, farms like tiny toys scattered along its sides, trees, sheep, houses and cattle glimpsed for only a moment before the plunge into the next tunnel, leave a sense of having looked for an instant through some magic door to see a bit of an unreal world. From boy-hood this glimpse has been for the author the most thrilling moment of the journey, a flashlight view of a remote dale, waited for with tense intention to see more than last time and to impress a picture on the memory. In the years when at last one could walk the length of this remote dale, explore its river and tributary gills, learn to know its farms and people and to hear, see and discover its life and history, it lived up to all the alluring promise which imagination had built upon the swift glimpses of youth. Today one can understand what moved the eighteenth-century surveyor to his most unusual enthusiasm.

We might think that, except for the distant sight of the expresses roaring across the high fellside at the dale head, Dent had never heard the sounds of industrial life. Though never on an urban scale, Dent has had its close acquaintance with industry and signs of this add an interest for that delight-ful character of the nineteenth-century writers, 'the curious traveller'. Marble quarrying, cutting and polishing, coal mining and textiles have all had their share in the life of the dale, but their harshness has been ameliorated and their traces do not obtrude.

Dentdale – among the older inhabitants the whole dale is usually called Dent with no further qualification, the village being invariably Dent Town – has been fortunate in having some inhabitants and visitors who combined their love of the dale and its folk with a capacity for powerful writing. They have pictured its life for us at the turn of the eighteenth and the early nineteenth century in words that make its people live again. At the opening of the nineteenth century Dent was still larger than Sedbergh, the nearest town, and both post-town and polling station for the area. The construction of two turnpike roads, which began in 1761 with an Act for repairing the road between Kirkby Stephen through Sedbergh to the Greta Bridge on the way to Lancaster and from Askrigg through Sedbergh to Kendal, started a growth in Sedbergh and a consequent decline in Dent. There was no important road through Dent – no way out at the head but by a mountain-ous track on to the wild moors of Newby Head, or by Deepdale

through a mountain pass over 1,550 ft into Kingsdale and the
Ingleton district.

The dominant position of Dent Town in the affairs of this
corner of Yorkshire has its roots in events far back in history.
It was a British village and the centre of a district never settled
by Angles, Danes or Normans, but receiving in the tenth and
later centuries a considerable influx of Norsemen. Its early
lords, Arkel and Aykfrith, were comrades of Cnut and the
wide area of the lordship of Dent, then established, persisted
long after the founding of Sedbergh with its small Norman
castle and its position as a dependant of the Norman manor of
Whittington. After centuries of independence the lordship
was forfeited to the Crown and, like Kettlewell and other
manors, was later sold to investors and then to the tenants who
became freeholders. From 1485 to 1629 Dent had been a Crown
manor, from 1629 to 1670 in secular hands, then in 1670 it was
transferred to freeholds and the Twenty Four Sidesmen of
Dent took over the lordship. It is thought that 'sidesmen' is a
corruption of 'synodsmen', coopted and not elected.[2]

The farms are nearly all small freeholds and their occupants
are a sturdy race of people, independent of mind and action,
who took a leading part in the Pilgrimage of Grace and among
whom George Fox found many of his early followers when
Quakerism sprang up in these parts.

Dent first came to the notice of the 'polite' world when the
poet Robert Southey published his miscellany *The Doctor*,
1834–7. By the accident of the relation of one of his servants to
a family which had moved out of Dent, he was able to collect
from the older folk stories of life in Dent during the third
quarter of the eighteenth century. The most impressive part of
these stories was the detailed picture of the knitting industry,
of the preoccupation with what he called 'the terrible knitters
of Dent', and of the knitting schools in which the youngest
children were taught to knit. Although the industry was
common to much of the dales (see Chapter Six p 98) the phrase
'terrible knitters' has adhered in popular writing and memory
to Dent only.

A writer with a closer personal connexion was Mary Howitt,

who with her husband, William, made long visits to her many
Quaker relations in Dent. Legends and memories collected
among her older friends were used as the basic material in
her novel *Hope on; Hope ever*, a book now eagerly sought and
highly treasured throughout the dale. This story was located
at and around Gib's Hall, two miles above Dent Town, and is
an acceptable record of life in the dale. William Howitt included Dent in his *Rural Life of England*, 1838, and together
these books brought Dent, with the knitters of every age-
group of the population, into the realm of literary tradition.
This literary discovery was not, however, comparable with the
topographic discovery of the other dales which was described
in the last chapter. The accounts of these three writers can be
taken as the prelude to a very analytical description of life in
the area which was written towards the end of his life by Adam
Sedgwick (1785–1873).[3]

For many generations the Sedgwicks had been 'statesmen',
small freehold farmers in the dale, and Adam's father was
vicar of Dent for fifty-four years. Adam was educated at the
grammar school which stands, an attractive building now put
to other uses, in a corner of the churchyard; it was built and
endowed by the freeholders of the parish in 1603. He became
skilled in mathematics, Latin and Greek, but his greatest
joy was to tramp the fells and explore the gills of his dale, to
talk with the old men and absorb the history and the lore of the
area, learning all that he could at the same time of the wild
life which was then so abundant. At the age of sixteen he went
to Sedbergh School, then at nineteen he entered Trinity
College, Cambridge. He became a Fellow there in 1810 and in
1818 was appointed Woodwardian Professor of Geology. His
career as a geologist was outstanding and he ranks as one of the
greatest pioneers of the subject in this country. During all his
academic career he remained in close contact with Dent, visiting it whenever he could and taking an interest in its affairs.

Three and a half miles above Dent Town, Cowgill Beck
joins the Dee at a place called Cowgill or Lea Yeat. At the
beginning of the nineteenth century Sedgwick says, 'the poorer
inhabitants of the hamlet [he is speaking of Cowgill] especially

those in the remoter parts of it, were without instruction, of
reckless life and without the common comfort and guidance of
social worship in the house of God.' Through the efforts of
Mrs John Sedgwick and some others a small chapel at Cowgill,
which had been built first by the Sandemanians, was taken over
and dedicated, after rebuilding, as Cowgill Chapel. The
documents relating to it and its consecration were sent to the
Bishop of Ripon's secretary, but nearly thirty years later the
trustees learned that these documents had never been regis-
tered, and protest and action had to be taken to secure the
righting of this grave oversight.

When registration was properly made in 1865 a further
mistake had changed the name to 'the District and Chapelry
of Kirkthwaite'. To secure the restoration of the true and
older name of Cowgill Chapelry, Adam Sedgwick wrote and
published the unique *Memorial by the Trustees of Cowgill
Chapel*, with some appendices published later as a second
volume. In these two slim volumes he collects the history and
social character of the area and gives a very full and lively
account of the customs of the dalesfolk in a way which has
been done for few other parts of Britain. He explains at great
length that the correct name of the part of the dale above
Cowgill is *Kirthwaite* and that the letter 'k' is an unwarranted
intrusion into a Norse name. He speaks of the history and the
climate of the area. Transport was difficult, supplies of wool
came into the dale by long trains of pack ponies, and butter
was taken out with the knitted goods. Life was hard, but
Sedgwick rejoiced in the strong fellowship which bound the
folk together.

Speaking of Dent Town he says of its old quaint street,

I regret the loss of the grotesque and rude, but picturesque
old galleries, which once gave character to the streets; and
in some parts of them almost shut out the sight of the sky
from those who travelled on the pavement. For rude as
were the galleries, they once formed a highway of communication to a dense and industrious rural population which
lived on flats or single floors.

Of the people he says:

> Their social habits led them to form little groups of family
> parties, who assembled together in rotation, round one blaz-
> ing fire, during the winter evenings. This was called
> *ganging a sitting* to a neighbour's house ... Let me try to
> give a picture of one of these scenes in which I have myself
> been, not an actor but a looker on ... there was a blazing
> fire in a recess of the wall; which in early times was com-
> posed of peat and great logs of wood. From one side of the
> fireplace ran a bench, with a strong and sometimes orna-
> mentally carved back, called a *lang settle*. On the other side
> of the fire-place was the Patriarch's wooden and well carved
> arm-chair; and near the chair the *sconce* adorned with crock-
> ery. One or two small tables, together with chairs or benches
> gave seats to all the party there assembled ... They took
> their seats; and began the work of the evening, and with a
> speed that cheated the eye they went on with their respective
> tasks ... by way of a change some lassie who was bright
> and *renable* was asked to read for the amusement of the
> party. She would sit down, and, apparently without inter-
> rupting her work by more than a single stitch, would begin
> to read – for example, a chapter of *Robinson Crusoe*. In a
> moment the confusion of sound ceased and no sound was
> heard but the reader's voice and the click of the knitting
> needles. Or on another and graver party, some one, perhaps,
> would read a chapter from the *Pilgrim's Progress*. It also
> charmed all tongues to silence but, as certainly, led to a
> grave discussion so soon as the reading ceased.

Sedgwick's Memorial came to the attention of Queen Vic-
toria and a short Act of Parliament at last established the
Chapelry of Cowgill within Dent parish.

The coal trade was very active in Sedgwick's time; he gave a
good deal of notice to it, and his description of the coal carts
and the old methods of carting has already been quoted (p
86). While the Garsdale and other collieries were for a time
connected with the burning of lime, they had a steady role in the

provision of house coal until well into the second half of the nineteenth century. The great geologist John Phillips, contemporary of Sedgwick, to whom we owe so much of our knowledge of the basic geology of the Yorkshire Pennines, summarized in volume II of his *Geology of Yorkshire*, 1836, when describing the rocks of the western part of Yorkshire gave the name 'Dent Marble Group' to the limestones of the lower part of what he named the Yoredale Series. This name was given because the limestones from Hardraw Scar and Simonstone to Underset were all being quarried in and around Dentdale and were cut and polished for marble. This was the first official use of the term Dent Marble. Similar rocks in Weardale, County Durham, provided the 'Frosterley Marble' which was cut and polished for use in Durham Cathedral, and other comparable limestone was used in Egglestone Abbey from the bed of the Tees. The earliest use of polished limestone in our area, however, was noted about the end of the seventeenth century.

The quarries from which the marble was got are widely scattered around the valley and in the little side gills, most of them now overgrown, but in their refuse hillocks it can still be seen that three kinds of limestone were used. One is a very dark colour, black when polished, containing abundant fossils mainly of corals, often of large size. There is another 'black' marble almost free of fossils, and there is a third variety in which, in a grey background, there is an abundance of fossil crinoids, 'sea lily' stems and fragments. Quarries are known to have been at work by the middle of the eighteenth century, but it was not until the later years of the century that quarrying became organized as an industry. The limestones are all well bedded and split into beds of varying thickness, some thin, some thick. Also the limestones are jointed and tend to break along vertical joints into rectangular masses. Limestone could thus be worked, when exposed in the quarry, by using only levers and wedges to get up blocks, no explosives being used as these might shatter and make weak spots which would spoil the polish. The blocks were cut to size by hand saws in the quarry, the saws being broad, long blades of iron with small corrugations, held in a frame and pushed back and forth while being fed with water and sharp sand. About the turn of the century the saws were worked by water-wheels at the High Mill in Arten Gill, near the head of the dale. High Mill had been built during the first half of the eighteenth century for carding and spinning wool. In 1780 and again in 1800 it is mentioned as a woollen mill, but by 1812 it was described in a lease as a 'marble mill'. The ruins of the mill, or rather its foundations, can still be found just below the magnificent Arten Gill viaduct. At the foot of the gill there is the Low Mill, which may also have been a yarn-spinning mill but which by 1800 was used for polishing black marble. In 1815 the Low Mill was extended and sawing by power was added to the polishing work being done.

The High Mill claims the interest of some engineers through its second water-wheel. This wheel was partly made of iron and had been made to drive spinning jennies; it was sixty feet in diameter. William George Armstrong, the founder of Armstrong's great engineering works on Tyneside, married Margaret Ramshaw in 1834 when he was twenty-four years old, and the following year took her for a holiday in Yorkshire during which he spent some time in Dent to enjoy the fishing in the Dee. During his wanderings he came across the marble works with its huge water-wheel enclosed in a two-storey building, driving sawing and polishing machinery. He may have known of the works before his visit, as his contemporary and friend in Newcastle, John Blackmore, a civil engineer, was the son-in-law of the owner of the marble works. However it came about, Armstrong's visit to the works proved to be of momentous interest. After inspecting the machinery he traced the stream to its source, examined and estimated the size of its springs, its fall and so on, and tried to calculate the available power. He came to the conclusion that the wheel was using efficiently only about a twentieth of the available power. On his return to Newcastle the memory of the days in Arten Gill turned his thoughts to the more efficient use of water power, and from this sprang his preoccupation with hydraulic machinery.

In 1838 he submitted his first scientific paper on water

power and also made, in the High Bridge works of Henry
Watson, a rotary hydraulic machine.

This was the beginning of the interest and fertile invention
in hydraulic machinery from which grew the Armstrong works.
Before his visit to Dent Marble works Armstrong had been
articled to a solicitor, Armourer Donkin, and in 1835 he
became a partner in Donkin's firm. After the visit and his
studies of water power, he rapidly became one of the foremost
engineers of his day and turned from the law to his own
business.

About the time of Armstrong's visit the marble works were
expanding and their trade was well established. The polished
marble was sent out as slabs for monuments, fireplaces and
small articles of a wide range of types. Little has survived from
the works except a few order books, but these will give some
indication of the trade during the few years to which they
refer.[4] By 1840 the trade was well organized as a processing
company, buying the marble in slab from the quarries but
not running the quarries directly.

1840 Apl. 8
4 Blk m. chimneypieces designs 1, 2, 3, & 4 @ 30s
1 Blk do. No. 5. @ 94s 6d
1 Vein do. No. 6. @ £5 10s od
1 Blk do. No. 7. £3 10s od. to John Inman of Newcastle.

Although the pattern books have not survived, such an account
as this one shows a very wide range of pattern when a fireplace
can vary between 30s (£1.50) and 110s (£5.50).

Mble Monument for Mr John Inman put up in the Free
Sunday School which was built at his expence.
carriage to Sedbergh £5
Lettering 15 doz & 1 at 2s 6d per doz. £1 18s od.
Sent to Sedbergh by Jos Blaydes weighing 3c.2.7. case No. 2.
John Kirkbride, Carlisle, Cr.
By Troughton Tablet for the above Monument £1 8s. od
by cutting and blacking 15 doz & 1 letters £1 18s od

During the same month many chimneypieces and slabs were sent to various towns and the journeys must have been very difficult. Material was sent to Norwich – Thomas Parrington, carrier, saw it to Gargrave and from there it went by canal and sea. It is probable that the old road from the marble mill over Dent Head to Ribblehead would be used, and then down Ribblesdale to Settle and the Keighley to Kendal turnpike after that.

Five chimneypieces were sent to London. They went by carrier to Stockton-on-Tees, almost certainly using part of the Kendal to Askrigg turnpike, then were shipped on the schooner *Darlington*, Captain Tate, to Beale's Wharfe in the Pool of London, and there transhipped to a lighter. With other marble goods they were sent to Mr John Poulson, 13 Size Lane, London, who wrote later that, not having warehouse room ready, he had disposed of them at cost price less his commission – £31 8s (£31.40) less £3 2s 6d (£3.13) being £28 5s 6d (£28.28), a loss of £6 4s 6d (£6.23) on their price. Poulson later became a regular customer for fairly large quantities of chimneypieces, and after the completion of a new warehouse he took batches of twelve pieces at once. Another journey was the passage of fireplaces to Southport, going by carrier to Lancaster, then by canal to Preston. The handling of these heavy goods must have called for a high degree of skill on the part of the carriers.

Many masons were supplied with small pieces to order, in sizes which they supplied, and such things as mortars, artists' palettes, inkstands and other small goods were sold at quite small prices. A black marble mortar, $9\frac{1}{2}$ ins in diameter and 5 ins deep, was a pound.

1840 Oct. 30
to Rev John Sedgwick, Dent,
a Horton Flag 5 ft 11 in × 31 in × 3 in for a gravestone £2 10s od
cutting 104 letters $1\frac{3}{4}$ & $144\frac{7}{8}$ – 248 @ 3d   £2 16s od (sic)
Dec. 28 To Rev Sedgwick for Cowgill Chapel, a font £5 os od

The trade was expanding through the next few years, and some sort of a catalogue was issued, as most orders are now given simply by a number. The principal market was divided between London and Newcastle, where there were warehouses. Some dealers' orders were of the type:

Mr. Charles Swift, Preston.
10 chimneys, Fossil, Vein and Black, Various sizes and from £1 10s 0d to £10 10s 0d.
The above prices to include carriage to Preston and are considered low owing to a desire to introduce the sale of Black & Fossil there. Mr. Swift to be allowed 5 per cent on sales.

New developments were made in the preparation of polished marble table tops and inlaid work in which the chief dealers were Messrs Ingram and Clarke of Liverpool. They took two dozen or more tops at a time and had them mounted in various styles by their own workmen. The vicar of Sedbergh had a chess table made, but this elaborate work was only charged at £3. It is not easy to get an accurate idea of the size of the trade. So far as the books go it would seem that in the three years 1842 to 1844 something like 420 chimneypieces were produced, the larger part of them for the warehouses at Newcastle, Sunderland and Darlington. The next largest amount went to London and a third important group to Liverpool.

When the railway came to Dent the trade had a further expansion as it was possible to dispatch goods more cheaply than by the old carting methods. This rise in demand, however, was neutralized to some extent by the introduction of Italian marbles which the Dent firm had occasionally to buy to suit a customer. For a short time the firm did quite a lot of polishing of Italian rough slabs for the trade.

The quarries had ceased to work and the marble works had closed down before 1900, and now most of the traces are grass-grown mounds on the fellsides and in the gill heads. The name Dent Marble, however, is an instant response, along with 'terrible knitters', when any mention is made of the dale. It has returned to a quiet country dale in which, even today, much of the hay crop is carried into the laithes by sledge, this still being the best vehicle for the steep fellsides; milk is still brought from the outlying shippon in a 'back can'; the dialect of the older people and most of the men is still rich with Norse words and phrases, and the dale still has a hidden wealth of deep rocky gills, attractive river scenery and abundant fine waterfalls. The neighbouring three dales, which have much in common with Dentdale, all have the vital difference of a main motor road through their length with all this means of noise and bustle. Although Dent is becoming better known, and cars are now traversing its whole length and over the top to Ingleton or Hawes, it still keeps all the character of 'the remote dale'.

Notes

Chapter One

1. A full account of the topography, geology and biology will be found in Raistrick, A. & Illingworth, J. *The Face of North West Yorkshire*. Dalesman, Clapham, 1949. Chapter 2.

Chapter Two

1. The most recent authoritative account of these settlements and the evidence to be derived from place-names is that in Smith, A. H. *The Place-names of the West Riding of Yorkshire*, Vol vii, Introduction. Cambridge, 1962.
2. *The returns for the West Riding of the County of York of the Poll Tax laid in the second year of the reign of King Richard the Second (AD 1379)*. Yorkshire Archaeological Society, 1882.
3. Dixon, J. H. *Chronicles and stories of the Craven Dales*. 1881. Whitaker, T. Dunham. *History and Antiquities of the Deanery of Craven*. 2nd ed. 1812.

Chapter Three

1. Printed in Vol 105 of *Yorkshire Archaeological Society, Record Series*. Three seventeenth-century surveys, 1941.
2. The earlier deeds are recited in the indenture of August 1st, 1902.
3. In the Central Reference Library, Bradford. *Kettlewell Byelaw Book, June 1777–1900*.
4. These leases are in the North Riding County Record Office, Northallerton, Accession ZT. I am indebted to the County Archivist for copies of them.
5. The material for Conistone is hitherto unpublished. It is contained in the large collection of deeds and MSS belonging to Miss Procter which is now catalogued by the National Register of Archives under the title 'Procter Records, Conistone, Yorkshire', and in a smaller collection of deeds among my own MSS. It is due to the kindness of Miss Procter that this material has been made available for study.

Chapter Four

1. The material for this chapter is taken almost entirely from the Procter Records.

Chapter Five

1. Hurtley, T. *A Concise account of some Natural Curiosities in the environs of Malham, in Craven, Yorkshire*. London, 1786.
2. Bray, W. *Sketch of a Tour into Derbyshire and Yorkshire*. 1782.
3. Craster, O. E. A medieval lime kiln at Ogmore Castle, Glamorgan. *Arch. Cambrensis*. CI. 72–6. 1951.
4. Smith, A. H. *The Place-names of the West Riding of Yorkshire*, vi. CUP, 1961.
5. Mortimer, J. *The Whole Art of Husbandry, or the Way of Managing and Improving Land*. 1st ed. 1707, quote from 3rd ed. 1712, iv, 68.
6. Young, A. *A Six Months Tour through the North of England*, IV, 482. 1770.
7. Hutton, J. *A Tour to the Caves in the Environs of Ingleborough and Settle*, 49. 1782.
8. Malham Moor mining MSS in author's collection.

Chapter Six

1. Raistrick MSS (mills) for Kettlewell and Malham mill deeds, etc.
2. Hartley, M. and Ingleby, J. *The Old Hand-knitters of the Dales*. Clapham, 1951.
3. Details of these wheels and their arrangements will be found, with maps, in Raistrick, A. 'The Mechanization of the Grassington Moor Mines', *Trans. Newcomen Soc*. 29, 179–93, 1955 and in Raistrick, A. & Jennings, B. *A History of Lead Mining in the Pennines*, 214–20, 1965.

Chapter Seven

1. A general account of these mining fields is given in Raistrick & Jennings, *op cit*.
2. William Brown's Letter Book, 137–40. MS in the collections of the North of England Institution of Mining Engineers, Newcastle upon Tyne.
3. Raistrick, A. Paper on mechanization already quoted.
4. Grassington to Pateley Bridge and Knaresborough turnpike papers in MSS collections at Skipton Library.

Chapter Eight

1. Raistrick, A. *Green Tracks on the Pennines*. Clapham, 1962.
2. Haldane, A. R. B. *The Drove Roads of Scotland*. Nelson, 1952.
3. Lancashire County Record Office. DD Ke 79.

Chapter Nine

1. Raistrick, A. & Gilbert, O. L. 'Malham Tarn House: its building materials, their weathering and colonization by plants', *Field Studies*, L. No. 5, 89–115. 1963.
2. Whitaker, T. D. *The History and Antiquities of the Deanery of Craven*, 38. 1812.
3. The material of this chapter is taken from a collection of autograph letters and transcripts of letters by Collins, along with MSS relating to the mines, in the author's MSS collection. Another collection of letters was in the possession of H. L. Bradfer-Lawrence but were not available for use. Since his death the final location of these letters is awaited with interest.
4. Raistrick, A. 'Mineral Deposits in the Settle-Malham District', *Naturalist*, 119–25, 1938. 'The Malham Moor Mines, Yorkshire', *Trans. Newcomen Soc.*, xxvi, 69–77, 1947–9. 'The Calamine Mines, Malham, Yorks', *Proc. Univ. Durham Phil. Soc.*, xi, 125–30, 1954.

Chapter Ten

1. The sparse details of this charity and fuller details of William Fawcett's charities are given in Return and Digest of Endowed Charities (W.R. of Yorkshire), made in August 1894, parish of Arncliffe.
2. This very lengthy indenture is printed in full in the *Bradford Antiquary*, Vol ii, 209 ff, 1894.
3. A Terrier of all the Houses Lands Annual Stipends belonging to the chapel and school at Halton Gill in the Year 1781, made by Thomas Lindley, Curate.
4. Shuffrey, W. A. 'Halton Gill in the Olden Time', Part II of *Littondale: past and present*. Archdeacon Boyd and Shuffrey, W. A. Leeds, 1893.
5. All the documents dealing with this inquiry are in the author's MSS collection.
6. The log book of the school has been used for the later period.
7. North Riding Record Office documents ZT and will of Philip Swale.
8. The log book has been used for the later period. See also Raistrick, S. E. 'A Dales Schoolmaster', *Dalesman*, xxi, 688–90. 1960.
9. For Hewitt and for Threshfield School before the log book, Hewitt's will and early school papers, etc, are in the Raistrick MSS.

Chapter Twelve

1. Quoted from *Paterson's Roads; . . . principal Cross roads in England and Wales*. Edward Mogg, 1826.
2. Much of the detail of Crowther's life is based upon Crowther's own account given in the 1920s when he asked the author, one of

his friends, to assist him with a possible autobiography. This idea was soon given up by Crowther, but I am glad to have this opportunity to use some of his material and to record my tribute to him.

Chapter Thirteen

1. Messrs Rennie, Broun and Shirreff. *General View of the Agriculture of the West Riding of Yorkshire with Observations on the means of its Improvement.* 1794. 111.
2. Thompson, W. *Sedbergh, Garsdale, and Dent; Peeps at the past history.* Leeds, 1892. 259.
3. Sedgwick, Adam. *A Memorial by the Trustees of Cowgill Chapel.* Cambridge, 1868.
   Sedgwick, Adam. *Supplement to the Memorial of the Trustees of Cowgill Chapel with an Appendix etc* printed in 1868. Cambridge, 1870.
4. Books of the marble works in Raistrick collection of MSS.

Index

THE MOST SOUGHT AFTER SERIES IN THE '70's

These superb David & Charles titles are now available in PAN for connoisseurs, enthusiasts, tourists and everyone looking for a deeper appreciation of Britain then can be found in routine guide books.

BRITISH STEAM SINCE 1900 W. A. Turpin   45P
An engrossing review of British locomotive development – 'Intensely readable' – COUNTRY LIFE. Illustrated.

LNER STEAM O. S. Nock   50p
A masterly account with superb photographs showing every aspect of steam locomotive design and operation on the LNER.

THE SAILOR'S WORLD T. A. Hampton   35P
A guide to ships, harbours and customs of the sea. 'Will be of immense value' – PORT OF LONDON AUTHORITY. Illustrated.

OLD DEVON W. G. Hoskins   45P
'As perfect an account of the social, agricultural and industrial grassroots as one could hope to find' – THE FIELD. Illustrated.

INTRODUCTION TO INN SIGNS
Eric R. Delderfield   35P
This beautifully illustrated and fascinating guide will delight everyone who loves the British pub. Illustrated.

THE CANAL AGE Charles Hadfield   50p
A delightful look at the waterways of Britain, Europe and North America from 1760 to 1850. Illustrated.

BUYING ANTIQUES A. W. Coysh and J. King   45P
An invaluable guide to buying antiques for pleasure or profit. 'Packed with useful information' – QUEEN MAGAZINE. Illustrated.

RAILWAY ADVENTURE L. T. C. Rolt   35P
The remarkable story of the Talyllyn Railway from inception to the days when a band of local enthusiasts took over its running. Illustrated.

A SELECTION OF POPULAR READING IN PAN

CRIME
Agatha Christie
| THEY DO IT WITH MIRRORS | 25p |

John D. MacDonald
| PALE GREY FOR GUILT | 25p |

Peter O'Donnell
| A TASTE FOR DEATH | 30p |

Dick Francis
| FLYING FINISH | 25p |
| BLOOD SPORT | 25p |

Ed McBain
| SHOTGUN | 25p |

Ronald Kirkbride
| THE SHORT NIGHT | 25p |

GENERAL FICTION
George MacDonald Fraser
| ROYAL FLASH | 30p |

Mario Puzo
| THE GODFATHER | 45p |

Rona Jaffe
| THE FAME GAME | 40p |

James Leasor
| THEY DON'T MAKE THEM LIKE THAT ANY MORE | 25p |

William Mitford
| LOVELY SHE GOES! | 30p |

Arthur Hailey
| HOTEL | 35p |
| IN HIGH PLACES | 35p |

Edwin Corley
| SIEGE | 35p |

Gordon Honeycombe
| NEITHER THE SEA NOR THE SAND | 30p |

Nevil Shute
| REQUIEM FOR A WREN | 30p |

Kyle Onstott
MANDINGO 30p
DRUM 35p
MASTER OF FALCONHURST 35p
Kyle Onstott and Lance Horner
FALCONHURST FANCY 35p
Lance Horner
HEIR TO FALCONHURST 40p

ROMANTIC FICTION
Georgette Heyer
COUSIN KATE 30p
FREDERICA 30p
BATH TANGLE 30p
Sergeanne Golon
THE TEMPTATION OF ANGELIQUE: Book One
The Jesuit Trap 30p
THE TEMPTATION OF ANGELIQUE: Book Two
Gold Beard's Downfall 30p
THE COUNTESS ANGELIQUE: Book One
In the Land of the Redskins 30p
THE COUNTESS ANGELIQUE: Book Two
Prisoner of the Mountains

HISTORICAL FICTION
Frederick E. Smith
WATERLOO 25p
Jean Plaidy
MADAME SERPENT 30p
THE WANDERING PRINCE 30p
GAY LORD ROBERT 30p
MURDER MOST ROYAL 35p
Colin Forbes
TRAMP IN ARMOUR 30p

NON-FICTION

THE PETER PRINCIPLE	Dr Laurence J. Peter & Raymond Hull	30p
THE AGE OF DISCONTINUITY	Peter F. Drucker	60p
SILENCE ON MONTE SOLE	Jack Olsen	35p
THE NINE BAD SHOTS OF GOLF (illus.)	Jim Dante & Leo Diegel	35p
HOW TO DRAW (illus.)	Adrian Hill	30p
THE SECRET OF FORETELLING YOUR OWN FUTURE	Maurice Woodruff	25p
THE UNQUIET MIND	William Sargant	45p
LIFE AT THE LIMIT (illus.)	Graham Hill	35p
HITCH-HIKER'S GUIDE TO EUROPE	Ken Welsh	35p
MISS READ'S COUNTRY COOKING	Miss Read	30p
RAVEN SEEK THY BROTHER	Gavin Maxwell	30p

Obtainable from all booksellers and newsagents. If you have any difficulty, please send purchase price plus 5p postage to P.O. Box 11, Falmouth, Cornwall. While every effort is made to keep prices low, it is sometimes necessary to increase prices at short notice. PAN Books reserve the right to show new retail prices on covers which may differ from the text or elsewhere.

I enclose a cheque/postal order for selected titles ticked above plus 5p a book to cover postage and packing.

NAME..

ADDRESS..

....

....